WIT

SOCIAL SKILLS AT WORK

David Fontana

SOCIAL SKILLS AT WORK

David Fontana

Problems in Practice

SOCIAL SKILLS AT WORK

David Fontana

Reader in Educational Psychology
University of Wales College of Cardiff

Published by The British Psychological Society
and Routledge Ltd.

First published in 1990 by The British Psychological Society, St Andrews
House, 48 Princess Road East, Leicester, LE1 7DR, in association with
Routledge Ltd, 11 New Fetter Lane, London EC4P 4EE, and in the USA by
Routledge, Chapman & Hall Inc., 29 West 35th Street, New York NY 10001.

British Library Cataloguing in Publication Data
Fontana, David
    Social skills at work. – (Problems in practice series)
    1. Personnel. Social skills
    I. Title II. Series
    302

    ISBN 1–85433–016–0
    ISBN 1–85433–015–2 pbk

Library of Congress Cataloguing-in-Publication Data available.

Printed in Great Britain by BPC Wheatons Ltd, Exeter

For Joyce and Cassy, in affection and thanks

Problems in Practice

This series is the natural successor to the popular *Psychology in Action* series, and continues and extends the aim of 'giving psychology away', that is, making psychological expertise more freely available.

Each title focuses on a common problem across a number of different professions – industry, education, medicine, the police and other public and social services. The approach is practical, drawing on examples from a range of work situations. And the reader is constantly invited to look at problems both as object and subject: accepting help as well as offering help; both giving and requesting expert advice. Psychologists have a great deal to say about how to improve our working lives and the aim here is to offer both practical skills and new insights.

THE AUTHORS AND EDITORS

Glynis Breakwell (Reader in Psychology, University of Surrey, Guildford)

David Fontana (Reader in Educational Psychology, University of Wales College of Cardiff)

Glenys Parry (Regional Tutor in Clinical Psychology, Knowle Hospital, Fareham and Top Grade Clinical Psychologist, Department of Psychotherapy, Royal South Hants Hospital, Southampton)

The original, problem-solving approach of this series was applied also to the creation of these titles, by a team of three, acting as both authors and editors. Each member of the team, drawing on their own practical experience, contributed ideas, material and criticism to every title, in addition to taking full responsibility for the writing of one or more of them. This approach ensures a book of wide practical relevance, combining the strengths and expertise of all authors, a uniformity of approach with a minimum of overlap between titles, yet retaining the clear, simple line of the single-authored book. The commitment of the authors to the series made all of this possible.

OTHER TITLES IN THE SERIES

Contents

4. EFFECTIVE COMMUNICATION

5. MANAGING CHANGE

Foreword

The 'Problems in Practice' series of books offers those working in the health and social services, industry and education practical advice on issues of fundamental concern to them in their work. The books are designed to show how psychological knowledge derived from a strong research base can be applied to problems faced in the professional management of people.

In *Social Skills at Work* David Fontana explores the way people relate to each other in their working lives and considers the routes by which people can achieve greater control over and safisfaction from them. This book is set apart from those manuals on social skills which offer mechanistic rules for improving your relationships. Fontana emphasises that true social skill is founded in self-knowledge: knowing how you feel in and understanding what you want from your exchanges with others, as well as understanding what they want from their relationships with you. He shows how it is possible to develop skills which are appropriate for you, and which do not rely upon artificial techniques which your true 'self' rejects, like the body reacts against a transplanted organ, and which can hinder its natural functioning. From first impressions to long-term work relationships, from one-to-one dialogue to operating in a group, Fontana asks you to analyse what makes you dissatisfied with your current habits of relating to others. With this self-knowledge as a starting point he suggests routes through to realistic change. Throughout he acknowledges the difficulties of managing change in a complex world of shifting social demands. Self-management comes to be seen as an integral part of social skill.

Ritualised or oversimplified recipes for effectively interacting with others are not offered. The practical examples, exercises and case studies which are a prime medium of explanation in the book are used to highlight its most important message: skill in handling other people, getting the most out of them and yourself, must begin with an understanding and acceptance of yourself for what you are and others for what they are.

Glynis Breakwell
Glenys Parry

Introduction

Much of professional life is concerned with human relationships. In fact for teachers, nurses, medical practitioners, social workers, managers, lawyers, ministers of religion, personnel officers, counsellors and a wide spectrum of similar professionals, human relationships are one of the key factors in determining the success or otherwise of professional performance. The purpose of this book is to explore these professional human relationships, that is, to look at how those of us involved professionally with others can get on better with them, and thus not only do our jobs more effectively but derive greater satisfaction and less stress from them.

As it's a practical book, the emphasis will be upon doing and understanding, rather than upon the examination of theoretical models of interpersonal communication. Though based upon the literature and upon research evidence, the book, as with the others in the 'Problems in Practice' series, will avoid detailed reviews of this evidence or of the literature in general. You the reader will be helped to examine central aspects of professional relationships, what you can give to and expect from these relationships, and why and how professional relationships sometimes go wrong. At the same time you'll be encouraged to look more closely at yourself, and to think more clearly about what goes on inside the psychological self during a relationship as well as what goes on outside.

The term 'social skills' is used throughout the book to refer to the way in which we can effectively manage our professional relationships. Because of its ubiquitous nature, there is no single accepted definition of this term, whether used in the context of personal or of professional life, but essentially it has to do with the effectiveness with which we communicate meaning or guidance or intention to others, and thus influence their behaviour or their potential behaviour. The way in which we exercise social skills depends both upon our own thoughts and feelings and upon the perception we have of the thoughts and feelings of those with whom we're communicating, and few of us are equally good at all of these skills. In the pages that follow, I'll be looking at the most important of these skills, and helping you clarify the way in which you think about and apply them.

The book should also help you contribute towards the development of appropriate social skills in others. In professional life we often work with clients and colleagues who find difficulty in relating well, not just with us but with most of the people they meet. Whether you want to help them at a formal or at an informal level (by running workshops or just by friendly words of advice), the book should give you some ideas on how to go about it.

Throughout the book, exercises, case studies and summaries are presented in order to give you a chance to reflect more closely upon your professional relationships and upon the problems that may arise within them. But the purpose of the book is not to lay down strict rules on what works and what doesn't work when relating to others. Good relationships have far more to do with concern and respect for other people and with a genuine understanding of why they behave as they do than with the application of set formulas.

Chapter One

What Are Social Skills?

RELATING TO OTHERS

Let's start with a few general factors associated with good professional social skills. These factors help to set the scene and to identify something of what we should and should not expect in our dealings with others. They help us to be realistic, and perhaps even to modify some of the demands we make upon *ourselves* as well as some of the demands we make upon the people with whom we work. Some of these factors will be returned to at various points during the book, allowing more extended discussion. Not all of them apply equally in all professional relationships as these relationships operate at a number of different levels (see page 11) and some are relevant to personal as well as professional encounters. But they indicate the mutual give-and-take that is a feature of successful interpersonal interactions.

1. We can't make an instant success of every professional relationship. But first impressions are important, and we need to work at them.

2. Even in the longer term, we can't expect everyone to like us. But if they dislike us we can expect to have some idea why, and whether the reason lies in ourselves or them.

3. There are plenty of people, both clients and colleagues, both superiors and juniors, eager to tell us by word or deed that we should be somebody we're not. In spite of them, we have the right to be ourselves in both professional and personal relationships.

4. Nevertheless we must accept that everyone is different, and that consistent with self-honesty we may have to vary our approach from one person to another.

FIRST IMPRESSIONS

BOX 1

Remembering names requires you hear the name properly in the first place. Ask for it to be repeated if necessary. Associate it with some real or imaginary feature of the owner's appearance or behaviour ('Mr Turner turns out his toes'). Make an exaggerated visual image of this feature and hold it in the mind for a moment. Use the name as often as possible in conversation. Remind yourself of it several times afterwards.

Holding one's own in a conversation depends upon having something to say. Research shows that people who talk easily (professional and socially) don't censor as vigorously their thoughts before speaking as do the tongue-tied. Few of us are short of thoughts. Be readier to give voice to them instead of automatically dismissing them as likely to be 'boring' or 'irrelevant' or 'facile'.

Self-disclosure should never be overdone in a professional relationship. The things you say could be held or used against you. But a readiness to say appropriate things about ourselves often encourages other people to open up too, and to feel they know and understand us better.

Praise and encouragement help people feel positive about themselves. Without being fulsome, there's usually something nice to say, for example appreciation of how the other person looks, or of their punctuality or of their accomplishments. Even 'Nice to see you again' or 'Thanks for coming' help establish the relationship.

Agreement gives a sense of friendship and common ground. Contrived and artificial agreement is rarely advisable, but most encounters start with some small talk about the weather or the swift passage of time or the state of the roads. Agreement over the sentiments expressed during this small talk helps prepare the atmosphere for weightier matters. Later in the conversation, agreement has more to do with seeing the other person's point of view, of acknowledging their difficulties, of recognising joint aims and objectives.

Research tells us that in most social interaction, whether personal or professional, some of the qualities that contribute to making a good first impression are:

- remembering names
- holding one's own in a conversation
- making appropriate self-disclosures
- giving praise and encouragement
- showing agreement.

EFFECTIVE RELATIONSHIPS

Other research studies suggest that long-term popularity goes with fairness, consistency, loyalty, honesty, a sense of humour, warmth, sympathy, and openness. The professional does not of course set out primarily to be popular, but to be effective and helpful. Nevertheless, these eight qualities are all likely to contribute towards successful professional behaviour. More specific studies into the role of professionals in caring professions such as nursing, social work and general medical practice, suggest that those who have good relationships with clients also:

- convey a respect for them and show an ability to listen
- put them at ease but avoid emotional over-involvement
- clarify the help that can and cannot be given
- accept justifiable criticism
- avoid undue exercise of professional power.

EFFECTIVE LEADERSHIP

Since many people in professional life are called upon to take the responsibilities of leadership, it's also useful to look at what research tells us about the effective leader. When working with a group, the successful leader has the ability to clarify issues, provide a feeling of group identity, stimulate discussion, cement intergroup relationships and provide consensus. In terms of personal qualities, the good leader is usually committed, objective, articulate, forceful, persuasive and initiatory, and able to keep a balance between task- and people-centredness.

It would be unrealistic to expect all these qualities to be present in all professional relationships all the time. And dependent upon circumstances, some of them will sometimes be more important than others. But they represent a framework within which the professional can give most help to their client, pupil or patient, and get in return maximum possible co-operation. Good relationships not only take a large part of the stress out of any professional task, since for the great majority of us it is much easier to work with people with whom we get on well than with people with whom we get on badly, but they also give us a better chance of influencing the behaviour of others for the good. They therefore make our job easier, and are worth regarding as part and parcel of the tools of our trade.

CAN SOCIAL SKILLS BE LEARNT?

The question is sometimes asked whether the qualities discussed earlier are things that can be 'learnt'. If they can be, then the questioner usually goes on to express some reservations about such learning, since it smacks a little of a contrived, rather manipulative approach to human relationships. It would suggest that we 'learn' social skills in order to exercise power over others and get what we want from them.

The answer is that although it certainly is possible to learn to be socially manipulative (and socially devious), this isn't what this book is about. Good professional relationships are concerned not with cynical social manipulation, but with a genuine concern for other people's present wellbeing and future achievements. As indicated above, good relationships involve respect for others from the outset. Some people argue that respect should be earned, not given freely. In fact it depends upon the object of our respect. If what we're respecting is a person's ability to do something well, then certainly that respect has to be earned. But if what we're respecting is another person's *life*, the common humanity they share with us, then no matter how inadequate or incompetent or obstructive they are, we must learn to respect that humanity. This is not always easy to do of course, but it's the very experience of that respect that draws many people to the 'caring' professions.

Another answer to questions on the desirability of 'learning' in the field of social relationships is that to a great extent it's there already. Of course it is possible that temperament may make some of us potentially more patient than others, more sensitive and concerned about people, more tolerant. It may make some of us more sociable, more ready to listen, more willing to share. But within the boundaries determined by temperament, relating well to others is essentially a learned skill.

Much of this learning takes place at a young age. From early social interactions with parents, caretakers, siblings and friends we learn what is acceptable and what is not. As we grow older this learning continues, much of it dependent simply upon opportunity. We may be lucky in having perceptive and sympathetic parents and teachers and school-friends, who are concerned to give us the life space and the sensible social guidelines we need. Or we may learn at the hands of people who care little for our individuality and wellbeing and very much for their own.

So when we talk about 'learning' in the context of good social skills, we're discussing a process that has been ongoing virtually since birth, but doing so in a more positive and potentially constructive way. We're referring to some of the insights into social skills that are professionally helpful to us and which otherwise we might be left to learn, at best, through trial and error. There is nothing artificial or contrived about learning of this kind. Instead of the imposition onto the individual of alien social behaviours, it involves the development in him or her of potentialities and skills that have hitherto had scant encouragement.

AGE, STATUS AND GENDER

There are of course important differences in what constitutes 'good' social skills across age groups and across status groups. What is appropriate for a child isn't appropriate for an adult for example, and what is appropriate for a junior colleague isn't necessarily appropriate for a senior. In each case, social constraints and recognised practices dictate what is acceptable and what isn't. Rightly or wrongly, an adult can say something to a child and a manager can say something to a worker that wouldn't be acceptable if offered the other way around.

Without wishing unduly to upset this order of things, it's important to be properly critical of it. Children don't especially want or need to be subservient to adults all the time, or junior colleagues to senior. And often this subservience retards personal development in a child and professional development in a colleague. We need to stress repeatedly to ourselves if we work with children that those qualities which can make a child seem 'difficult' at times (for example, independence, strength of will, creativity, courage, outspokenness) are the very qualities that we admire most in adults. Related to this, an inclination in professional life to keep juniors in their place may have more to do with defending our own professional position and our own egos than with the abilities of the juniors concerned or with the best interests of the organisation for which we all work.

There are also significant differences in what is acceptable behaviour for men and women, with women able to say things to each other in public that would be looked at askance if said between men (for example terms of endearment), and men able to say things to each other that would be regarded as indelicate in women (for example nicknames and sexually explicit language). Similarly language *between* men and women can be significantly different from that used within either of the sexes, particularly where the relationship is an intimate one. Cultural factors also play a part here; for example the kiss is an acceptable formal greeting between men in certain cultures, but not in others. Some of these gender-related and culturally-related differences are rightly much less important now than once they were, but they are still with us, and can have an important influence upon the success or otherwise of a professional relationship.

The point to stress is that in professional relationships men don't have to be identified always with 'hard' masculine qualities and women with 'soft' feminine ones. Men can and should be just as capable as women of sensitivity and compassion where appropriate, and of the arts of co-operation and persuasion, while women should be just as capable as men of self-assertion and leadership and of the arts of competition and direction. These issues will be discussed later in their own right, but research shows that a large part of these sex-related behaviours are learnt. Children are usually taught (formally and informally) that dominance and aggression are tolerated and even admired in men, while submission and docility are encouraged in women.

This ambivalence can result in an imbalance in both personal and professional relationships, with men incapable of responding to the emotional needs of clients, pupils or patients as well as colleagues, and women incapable of responding to the need of others for challenge and focus. In exploring our expertise at professional relationships, it is important that we examine the sexual stereotypes that lie behind our behaviour, and explore ways of freeing ourselves from them. Equally, we need to explore the ways in which colleagues, clients and other people involved in our professional relationships serve to constrain us within these stereotypes. Since no one else has the right to live our lives for us, we have the right to object to these constraints.

POOR PROFESSIONAL RELATIONSHIPS: TONY AND BRENDA

Individuals who lack opportunities to develop their social skills do not always come from backgrounds that are clearly socially deprived or restricted. Nearly all of us have acquired some social relationship problems with which to contend. Let's take a typical example.

▢ *Tony has been working for four years as a personnel officer with a large manufacturing company in the Midlands. He has a good honours degree in psychology, and was married 18 months ago to a girl he met in the first year of his*

THE SOCIAL SKILLS WORKSHOP

BOX 2

The kind of social skills workshop attended by Tony provides opportunities for groups of professional people to get together over a day or two and examine their social problems. During the workshop, with the help of the leader and the other participants, they are prompted to identify such things as:

- the real nature of these problems – hitherto they may have misread them out of prejudice perhaps, or fixed ideas;

- the cause of the problems – does it lie in them or in others? What lies behind the cause?

- the solution to the problem – there's *always* a better way of handling a relationship that's going badly;

- a detailed description of the actual skills needed to bring about this solution;

- practise of these new behaviours through role-play exercises.

The workshop operates in an atmosphere of mutual support and understanding. No one is immune from social problems, so in a sense all are equal. No labels are assigned. Participants discuss each other's social difficulties but avoid expressions like 'you're too aggressive', or 'too shy', or 'too dishonest with people'. The emphasis is upon what people do and should not do, rather than upon what they are or what we think they are.

The workshop may consist of separate individuals or of a team of people (such as a management team). Activities during the workshop consist of discussion groups, role-play exercises, and appraisal and self-appraisal activities.

Ideally there is a follow-up workshop days or weeks later at which participants can report and assess progress.

university course. He describes himself as reasonably confident and extraverted, generally optimistic in his approach to life, and happy in his job and in his marriage. Yet when asked why he decided to attend a series of workshops dealing with professional and personal relationships he confessed that:

> I always get the feeling there's something missing in me. I'm reasonably popular with the people at work. But I never feel I get really close to them. Maybe deep down I don't trust anyone. Even with Jean my wife, I'm wary much of the time. When I'm asked direct questions about myself I usually hedge.
>
> As a personnel officer I need people to trust me, but I get the feeling they're a bit wary of me. Maybe they respond to my own lack of trust. Even if people talk to me about major problems in their lives it all seems to happen on the surface. My psychology degree certainly didn't teach me how to get rid of the barriers between myself and others. Perhaps that was my own fault. It's only recently I've been able to see those barriers. When people come to me for help I act as if I know all the answers, but I'm beginning to feel a fraud.

☐ Let's take another example. Brenda is an office manager, with considerable on-the-job experience and with wide responsibilities, both professional and personal, for the sizeable office staff in her organisation. She is separated from her husband, and lives with her teenage son and daughter. When asked the same question as Brian she responded with:

> Most of the stress in my job comes from trying to handle people. We have a fairly rapid turnover of staff in the office, so it's hard to get to know most of them really well. But I'm always having rows with someone or other. I try being hard, and I try being sweetness and light, and neither seems to work. If I get tough they resent it and fight back, and if I'm nice they think I'm weak and just take advantage of me.
>
> My problems at home don't help. Both my children seem to resent the time and energy I put into my job, and this makes me feel I'm failing them. I'm seriously thinking of resigning and taking on something less demanding. But I already feel a failure at the personal level, and if I quit now I'll have failed professionally too.

So what is going wrong? Both Tony and Brenda are apparently successful professional people, with job specifications which involve handling and relating to other employees, yet neither feels on top of the job. Tony's difficulties have to do with a defensiveness which he senses in himself, and which gets in the way of being open with others and of allowing them to be open with him. Notice how he says 'I act as if I know all the answers'. This suggests he feels he *should* know all the answers, and can't face admitting when he doesn't. He's insecure about himself and about his ability at the job, and needs help in sorting out why and what to do about it.

Brenda's problems are connected with her inability to sum other people up accurately and relate to them as individuals. She's trying to operate a blanket approach of being tough or of being nice to everyone, and obviously that isn't going to work. Like many women in her position, she also has divided loyalties between home and work, and again like many women she ends up feeling guilty about it, and bad about herself.

These two case studies demonstrate that neither appropriate academic and professional qualifications (as in Tony's case) nor lengthy work experience (as in Brenda's) necessarily mean we have mastered the skills and understanding essential if we are to relate well to those for whom we carry professional responsibility. The Tonys and Brendas of this world are by no means atypical. For many professionals there is a temptation to feel that just because they are qualified and have got on well in their careers, they are *ipso facto* good at handling clients or those who work for them. So if things go wrong, it is the other person who is to blame. But where Tony and Brenda score over many of those with similar problems is in their ability to accept that things are not well, and that the fault may lie with themselves and not automatically with others.

- To admit we're not always good at handling people does not mean we're professional failures; it means that by recognising we have some important learning to do we've taken an important step towards professional success.

- Once the need for this learning is recognised, the learning itself need present no insuperable difficulties.

PROFESSIONAL RELATIONSHIPS AT DIFFERENT LEVELS

So far I have talked generally about professional relationships, but there are of course a number of different levels at which these relationships operate, each of which requires a different kind of approach. The casual (though still professional) relationship we have with those colleagues with whom we only come into peripheral contact is very different from that which we have with those who work close to us, which is different again from that which we have with clients, students or patients. It's useful to summarise the various levels as follows:

Level 1: Peripheral relationships with porters, switchboard operators, office cleaners and anyone else whose job is not directly related to ours.

Level 2: Superordinate relationships with those working under us or directly answerable to us.

Level 3: Equality relationships with colleagues on the same grade or doing the same job as ourselves.

Level 4: Subordinate relationships with those working over us or to whom we are directly answerable.

Level 5: Client-orientated relationships with those who are professionally dependent upon us.

These levels are not in any absolute hierarchical order. But whereas the skills needed to make a success at Level 1 are relatively straightforward, those from Level 2 onwards become increasingly complex. It is sometimes argued though that the ability to get on well with others at Level 1 can be a touchstone of one's likely success at higher levels (in particular Levels 2, 3 and 5). If this argument is true, it is probably because the qualities required for success at Level 1, although straightforward, are amongst the most important and operate at all of the higher levels. For example, looking again at the list on page 5, it is clear that respect for others, the ability to listen to others, to put them at ease, to avoid status battles with them, and to show honesty and consistency, are qualities of value in relating to people at all levels. The sensitive professional realises this, communicates due appreciation and understanding, and helps facilitate the right kind of professional relationships.

How is this communication done? First and foremost by noticing the value of the Level 1 colleague concerned. One of the supposed hallmarks of good servants in days gone by was their unobtrusiveness. But realistically, we most of us like to be noticed. If people act as if we're not there, this suggests we're of no significance. So a smile or a word of two of greeting when we see a colleague reassures him or her that they matter. Sailing past them without a nod or a wave indicates to them we view their importance roughly on a par with the office furniture. Second by verbal appreciation for their contributions to professional life. 'Thank you' doesn't require much effort to say, but the parsimony with which some people use the phrase suggests it's more exhausting than a half marathon. Third by showing interest in their personal lives. People are always pleased to know you remember their hobbies or the names of their children or where they went on their holidays last year. Fourth by listening at least sometimes when they want to talk. If we never have time to spare for a person it suggests we think very little of them (the very expression 'I've no time for him or her' is significant here), and I return to this point later when discussing the art of being a good listener. And fifth by doing whatever we can to help put right the many grievances and injustices that people in low-status occupations have to face. Often these grievances seem small to us, but to the person concerned they loom like mountains. Sometimes a word in the appropriate place puts things right for them. But if there's nothing concrete we can do, at the very least we can explain why and offer our sympathy.

SELF-ESTEEM

What we are in fact doing is helping to build up the self-esteem of the Level 1 colleague. Low self-esteem is one of the major (some argue *the* major) factor in much psychological ill health and emotional suffering. At all five levels of relationship, the successful professional is a person who can enhance the self-esteem of the person with whom they are working. Not by flattery or exaggeration, but by encouragement rather than by discouragement, by emphasising what people can do rather than what they can't, and by showing the general respect and interest which I've already discussed.

Whilst on the subject of self-esteem, it is relevant to stress that what we've said about its importance in others applies equally to ourselves. Both Tony and Brenda in the examples given above have problems with self-esteem, linked in Tony's case to insecurity and in Brenda's to guilt. Low self-esteem leads us to:

▶ undervalue ourselves, especially in comparison with others;

▶ overcriticise ourselves and fall victim to perfectionism;

▶ possess a particular fear of failure, and sometimes set ourselves unrealistically high or low goals (on the basis that we can't be blamed if we fail to reach the high goals, and we can't fail if we aim for the low);

▶ feel too keenly the need for approval and to be liked;

▶ risk being overconformist ('My opinions must be wrong if they're out of step with everyone else's').

Note that self-esteem is not the same thing as conceit. Conceited people may in fact have very low self-esteem, and use an exaggerated view of their own importance as a way of defending against it. Self-esteem basically means self-acceptance, accepting and valuing ourselves and our abilities and emotions instead of continually punishing ourselves. Paradoxically, people who learn to accept themselves for what they are often find it easier to change than people who don't. Through self-acceptance they come to know themselves better, and to be objective about the need for change and how to go about it.

If you have trouble with self-esteem, start rewarding yourself more (by verbal backpats or in more tangible ways) for the things you *can* do. Worry a little less about what other people think (or what you *think* they think) about you. Learn from your mistakes instead of punishing yourself for them. Make some of the same allowances for yourself that you make for others.

Chapter Two

How Well Do You Know Your Social Self?

QUESTIONS TO ASK

Here are two sets of questions based upon the things people can usefully ask themselves when examining the quality of their professional social skills. Respond to both sets as openly and as objectively as possible, without feeling guilty if the answers seem unflattering. The questions are simply there to help self-reflection. The first set is related to the general ability to get on with others.

? *Am I socially successful?* A useful yardstick here is whether people are usually pleased to see me and vice versa, or whether there are people who I consistently try to avoid or who consistently try to avoid me.

? *With what kind of people do I get on well?* Do I relate well to most people or only to particular kinds? Do I relate best to people who are like me or unlike me, to equals or only to my seniors or juniors? To both sexes or only to one?

? *With what kind of people don't I get on well?* Is there a particular kind of person with whom I'm usually at odds? What is it about them that makes things difficult? Is it negative qualities in them, or do they in some way make me feel inadequate?

? *What is it that prevents me from relating well to some people?* Do I make an effort to get on with someone I dislike, or do I prefer not to bother?

? *Are there people who actively dislike me?* If so, who are they? Clients? Juniors? Colleagues? Why do they dislike me? Are they justified or simply being over-sensitive? Does their dislike bother me?

? *Are there people in my life who really understand me?* Understand my aims in life and why I'm the way I am? Understand my bad points as well as my good?

? *Are there people in my life who really accept me?* If they can't accept me, why is this?

? *Have I particular ways of behaving, or mannerisms, which others dislike?* If so, how important are these things to me? Are they worth the dislike of other people? Can I change them?

? *Am I moody?* Do people find me unpredictable and inconsistent? Do I carry problems from my private life into my professional life, and vice versa?

? *Are there people in my life with whom I'm really close?* Am I close only to my family? Have I personal friends? Professional friends? If I'm close to no one, why is this?

? *Am I prepared to learn from others?* Do I feel I'm usually the one who's in the right, or can I look objectively at issues? Can I acknowledge when I'm wrong? Can I accept it when people tell me unwelcome things about myself? Can I compromise?

? *Can I forgive people?* If I can't, why not? Do I secretly enjoy my resentment? Or the feeling I'm punishing the other person?

? *Do I lose my temper easily with others?* Anger may sometimes be justified, but does anger always require loss of temper? Does losing my temper help? How do I feel about it afterwards?

? *Do I always look for ulterior motives behind other people's behaviour?* Do I prejudge or do I try to be objective?

? *Finally, if I had to choose a best friend, would I choose me?*

The next set of questions relates more specifically to professional life:

? *Am I fair to the people over whom I have power or responsibility?* Would I like to work under myself? If not, do I expect too much from others? Do I secretly enjoy making their lives difficult?

? *Do I often feel put down by colleagues?* Do I feel other people are given professional advantages over me? Promoted above my head? Do I get the blame when it belongs to others?

? *Am I nervous when meeting clients or senior colleagues for the first time?* If so, what am I afraid of? Do I lack confidence in my professional abilities?

? *If I experience professional failure or embarrassment, can I talk it over with colleagues and friends?* Or do I avoid discussing it through embarrassment? Or because discussing it makes me feel inadequate? Or because there's no one I trust?

? *If differences arise with clients or colleagues, do I try and resolve them there and then?* Or do I prefer to escape from conflict as soon as possible?

? *When clients or colleagues want me to spare time for them above the call of duty, do I usually manage it?* Or do I make excuses? Or make vague appointments I probably won't keep?

? *If I fall out with someone in professional life, do I behave coldly to them or avoid them as much as possible afterwards?* Or do I try to behave normally towards them?

? *Am I really interested in other people's problems?* Or do I only listen to them because it's my job?

? *When I have something unwelcome that has to be said to a client or colleague, do I say it as soon as possible?* Or do I put it off for as long as I can?

? *Is doing my job effectively the most important professional consideration?* Or is it being popular? Or avoiding difficulties?

As with the first set of questions, these professional queries help us reflect upon certain important aspects of our professional relationships. They're not part of a scale on which we gain a score of one kind or another which compares our social skills with those of our peers. They act simply as an aid towards self-knowledge. But if you feel you don't emerge too well from them, be comforted. Neither do many other people who think seriously about what they're doing.

The reason is that relating to people in professional life isn't easy. Those in professions such as counselling, social work, medicine, are relating to individuals or groups many of whom already experience grave difficulties with relationships and life in general. The responsibilities of people in these professions are so acute, and the demands made upon them by society so great, that it's hardly surprising they often end up feeling inadequate. The purpose of the questions above isn't to make you feel worse, but to help identify more clearly where things may be going wrong in your professional relationships, and why.

Continue this process of identification by looking at Exercise 1.

HOW OTHERS SEE YOU

It is only when other people confirm recognition of the changes in you brought about by exercises like Exercise 1 that you can be sure of your development. Everyone who works with you is forming opinions and making judgements about you all the time, and allowing their opinions and judgements to influence the way they behave towards you. Sometimes these differ greatly from the way you see and think about yourself, so what goes wrong? Is it the other people who are mistaken? Or are you failing to project yourself in the way you think you are?

PERSONAL DEVELOPMENT

EXERCISE 1

Write down all the qualities you'd like to see in each of these three people:

▶ A boss
▶ A colleague
▶ A friend

(These may include consistency in a boss, loyalty in a colleague, warmth in a friend.) Now put a tick by each of these qualities *you* possess.

Where desirable qualities are missing, how can you develop them? Have you become stuck in particular ways of hinking about yourself or in particular ways of behaving? The three people above were chosen because they represent three sides of the person we ourselves need to be in good professional relationships, sometimes at each of the five levels identified in the last chapter, sometimes at one or other of them. If we expect others to have these qualities, it's right to try to develop them in ourselves too.

Help their development by selecting one of the qualities you haven't ticked. Now think of a situation within the next day or so where you can practise it (see page 24 for more details about acting out). After practising it, analyse the experience. Did it feel natural or unnatural? If it felt natural, why don't you practise it more often? If it felt unnatural, why was this?

When you've practised one quality, pick another and carry through the same exercise. Don't assume that your qualities or lack of them, and the personality which they help constitute, are set in tablets of stone. Personality is a *process* not an object; a living dynamic system, not a fossilised edifice. A characteristic of living systems is change and growth, and personality is no exception. Personality changes and grows as time passes. By becoming more aware of this and of the ways in which you want your personality to develop, you can influence the direction of this change and growth.

A criterion used by some psychologists when discussing psychological maturity is that there should not be too great a gap between the way you see yourself and the way in which others see you. The absence of such a gap is also sometimes taken to be a sign of self-knowledge, the rationale being that if you are very much at odds with other people over the kind of person you are, then maybe you are guilty of self-deception.

SELF/OTHER ASSESSMENT: MIKE AND BRIAN

☐ *An example helps illustrate this. Mike is 32 years old, and has a managerial job with a large production company in the south of England. He likes his work, but is disgruntled by his lack of promotion and by the recent elevation of a junior colleague above his head. On a two-day management training course, both Mike and Brian (the senior manager to whom Mike is directly responsible) took part in a self/other definition exercise. In this exercise, participants are invited to choose from a list of adjectives those which they feel best describe their personalities, and then to attempt a similar exercise for each other. Each person can then examine his or her own adjectives and compare them with the ones that other people have chosen for them.*

A second stage to this exercise is to ask other people, on a 1–5 scale, to rate each individual on the adjectives he or she has chosen as self-descriptors. Thus if I have chosen 'charming' for myself, the other people in the group will each now rate me (anonymously if they wish) for charm by awarding me marks out of five.

Here is Mike's list, together with the score that Brian awarded him.

How Mike sees himself	How Brian rates Mike (marks out of 5)
punctual	5
hard-working	5
innovative	1
co-operative	2
polite	2
able	4
perceptive	2
outspoken	5
honest	5
humorous	1
loyal	1
friendly	2
confident	5
depressed	4

SEEING WHAT YOU WANT TO SEE

We tend to see in others what we want to see. This is one reason why so many professional and personal relationships prove unsatisfactory. We may start off with an idealised picture of the other person, and when we get to know them we discover they're not like that at all.

To avoid the worst of the mistakes that arise from this subjectivity,

- until you get to know people better, focus on what they *do* rather than upon your feelings about them;
- avoid the *halo* and *demon* effects respectively: the halo effect occurs when we get such a good impression of someone that we interpret all their subsequent behaviour positively; the demon effect is the reverse.

Disposition and situation. There's also sometimes a tendency to 'halo' self and 'demon' others. For example, we're all prone to attribute our own negative behaviour to the *situation* ('I was under pressure at work'; 'I wanted to tell him the truth but I knew it would upset him'), while in people whom we're neutral or less friendly we attribute it to *disposition* ('That's the kind of person he is'; 'She blurts things out without thinking'; 'He wanted to make me feel bad about it').

Describing self and others. Most of us also stereotype ourselves more positively than we do others. For example, we are more likely to attribute such things as sense of humour, honesty, good looks, objectivity and kindness to ourselves than to others.

And here is the list of adjectives that Brian chose for Mike.

How Brian sees Mike

bolshy
humorless
hard-working
honest
punctual
uncreative
insensitive
disloyal
confident
remote
defensive
reliable
inflexible
morose

Mike as seen by himself and Mike as seen by Brian look like two quite different people. What's gone wrong, and what does it tell us about Mike's failure so far to win the promotion to which he feels entitled? Brian agrees that Mike is hard-working, punctual, honest and reliable, but certainly doesn't see him as loyal or innovative or perceptive. So do Mike and Brian define these things differently? Or is Mike failing to project his desirable qualities in a way that Brian can recognise? Or is it possible he doesn't possess them after all?

And is it possible that what Mike sees as good qualities – his outspokenness and his self-confidence – may in fact be perceived more negatively by Brian? Maybe these are the things that Brian equates with what he terms Mike's bolshiness. Clearly Mike and Brian had some very serious talking to do.

USING SELF/OTHER ASSESSMENT EXERCISES
With the help of the group leader, Mike was prompted to look at those qualities to which he laid claim on his self-assessment list but in which Brian found him lacking. For example he was asked to write down three recent examples of his loyalty to the firm and to Brian, and at the same time Brian was asked to write down three examples of Mike's disloyalty.

When the exercise was complete, they each looked at and commented on what the other had written. One of Mike's examples was that he'd refused to apply for a job with a competing organisation even though invited to do so and given a strong hint that his application would be successful. Reading this, Brian claimed ignorance of the matter. Mike counterclaimed that he'd written Brian a memo about it, but Brian protested that the memo had never reached him, and went on to express surprise that Mike hadn't come and told him of the matter personally. Mike countered by saying that Brian didn't seem to encourage his juniors to go to him with anything other than strictly business matters, and after initial protests Brian accepted this and agreed to make himself more approachable in the future.

This opened up another important area of difference between Mike and Brian, namely whether the former was innovative and creative or not. Mike felt strongly that he was an ideas man, and that Brian didn't recognise this because he felt threatened by it, which led him to block Mike's promotion.

The exercise thus allowed Mike and Brian to see how they had been misinterpreting each other. Brian wasn't the only one at fault here, and Mike was helped to recognise that often he pushed his ideas by being too outspoken and critical. Both men learnt first that they weren't as good at judging other people as they had thought, and second that they weren't always sending out the appropriate social signals. Both expressed their readiness to try to change in future, and identified specific ways in which this could be done.

Identifying specific social skills in this way is much more effective than general resolutions to 'be more approachable' or to 'be more friendly' or to 'be more open'. The trouble with resolutions of this kind is that we don't really know what they mean. I may decide to be more approachable, but does my approachability mean being more approachable *now*, when I'm particularly busy? And does it mean being more approachable to person X, who takes up so much of my time unnecessarily, or only to person Y, whom I rather like and don't mind seeing more often?

So Mike and Brian identified exactly what they needed to do in order to relate better to each other and to their colleagues. By going public on this they entered into a mutual commitment and thus gave themselves more incentive to stick to their good intentions. Brian, for example, promised to introduce a system allowing those working under him to make written suggestions of any initiatives they felt were needed. He undertook to see each person individually about these suggestions, and to provide a written as well as a verbal account of what he planned to do about them. He also promised to introduce machinery for keeping people better informed about forward planning, and for consulting his junior managers more systematically before taking decisions that affected them.

Mike agreed to write out a careful definition of what he understood by loyalty to the company, to let Brian see it for comment, and then to abide by this written code.

RESOLVING MISUNDERSTANDINGS
Without the management training course Mike's career might well have remained stagnant, not because he lacks ability but because he didn't understand that he was giving other people the wrong impression of himself. As for Brian, he would have failed to get the best out of Mike, and perhaps out of the other members of his team as well. He confessed he'd become so preoccupied with production and with the *things* associated with his job that he'd tended to forget about the *people*. A naturally friendly and considerate man, he had systematically been denying a large part of himself in his hunt for greater business efficiency. As he himself said, he'd forgotten that in the end the company is there for its employees as well as simply to sell its products.

It is important to note that Mike and Brian were able to settle their professional misunderstandings without angry confrontation (which would have risked opening up yet more areas of misunderstanding). Given the right context, they were able to reach understanding because each saw that the other was not posing a threat to him.

Let's leave Mike and Brian with the satisfaction of knowing they now both feel they get on much better not only with each other but with their colleagues in general. Moreover, Brian's new approach to the personal relationships side of his managerial role has led to several significant improvements in work efficiency, and has prompted greater team spirit and a happier atmosphere all round.

SELF-IMAGE

There are however two riders concerning how others see us and how we see ourselves. The first is that other people are in a sense mirrors in which we see ourselves. If they regard us as effective professionally and personally, it's much easier for us to see ourselves in the same way. But a problem arises in that we can all too easily come to depend upon the admiration others may have for our efficiency, or upon the way in which they see us as fulfilling their needs (quite apart from the fact that, just as some mirrors distort and make us look smaller than we are, others magnify and make us look bigger). The result is that we begin to find our significance – even our identity – lies in their good opinion of us.

This is bad not only for us but for them as well. It means we develop a vested interest in being indispensable, and therefore a vested interest in prolonging other people's reliance upon us. (The issue of helping is returned to on page 42.) The result is that in managerial posts we may hang on to the levers of power when they should be given to someone else, and in the caring professions such as counselling and medicine we may hang on to our clients instead of helping them move towards freedom and independence.

The second rider is that sometimes the mirrors from which we can learn most are not those held up to us by our friends (it was a wise man who once said 'Have you noticed that all your friends like you?'). Friendly people tend to study our feelings, and make allowances for us. Unfriendly people don't. This means that while unfriendly people can often be unfair to us, their remarks can also sometimes come uncomfortably close to the truth. So although it's right and proper that we thank providence first and foremost for our friends, we should also spare just a little gratitude for our enemies.

IMPROVING SOCIAL SKILLS

Now look at Exercise 2 opposite, which is adapted from the exercise given to Mike and Brian.

SELF-EXAMINATION

Exercise 2 is concerned with the fact that in order to relate well to others, we must recognise certain important facts about ourselves. Other people's behaviour doesn't happen in a vacuum. When they relate to us, they are relating to *us*, to the people we are. Their behaviour towards us is a response, in no small measure, to our behaviour towards them. If I want to know why people are intimidated or confused or irritated by me, I need to accept that this says something about me as well as something about them. Relationships involve more than one person, each of whom contributes to success and failure.

One of the values of *acting out* desirable qualities is that by consciously changing your behaviour in this way you therefore begin to receive new kinds of feedback from people. They start to see you in a different way, and react towards you accordingly. Assuming this feedback is positive (people are more welcoming perhaps, or more forthcoming, or more helpful), it reinforces the value of the new behaviour and encourages you to maintain it.

In some ways this is simply an extension of normal behaviour. As

SELF-EXAMINATION

EXERCISE 2

Two people who know you well are discussing you. They use a
number of words which they feel describe you accurately. Look at
the following list, and select all those words you think they may
have used.

friendly	likeable	witty
helpful	sensitive	sarcastic
hasty	erratic	warm
communicative	happy	spiteful
cold	talkative	calm
open	unpredictable	well balanced
honest	devious	anxious
reliable	reliable	quick-tempered
secretive	selfish	forceful
humorous	punctual	unforgiving
depressed	well mannered	kind
creative	thoughtful	remote
slow	able	understanding
formal	mean	

You now have an outline profile of yourself. Supplement it by
selecting all those words you think they would not have used.
Look at this profile and see what it tells you. Are you happy with
the qualities you have? If not (and here we need to be specific once
more) write down the ways in which the qualities you dislike
manifest themselves. Think of specific examples.

Next, think about the qualities you don't have but would like to
have. How would these manifest themselves? As in Exercise 1,
can you act them out when you wish to do so, even if they don't
appear to come naturally to you? (That is, can you behave as if you
have the qualities concerned?) Try it. If you can, what is it that
stops you from acting out these qualities all the time?

indicated earlier, many of our social skills are learnt. We learnt them because they brought us 'rewards' (desirable results such as approval or avoidance of disapproval) in the past. In childhood and adolescence we experiment with a wide range of behaviours, generally retaining those that produce rewards and abandoning those that do not. In adult life, however, our behaviour usually becomes more fixed. We don't experiment so much, and we're reluctant to try anything (such as expressions of regard, offers of help, frank comments) that may produce an unpredictable response from others. 'Acting out' is largely a matter of ridding ourselves of this social conditioning, and experimenting once more with the qualities we would like to have.

The 'unnatural' feeling you may experience when acting out is often only that of uncertainty mixed with a little apprehension. 'What will people think?' 'Will I look foolish?' Provided you act out behaviour that you genuinely want to develop in yourself, it is likely to be potentially as 'natural' a part of your personality as many of the other things you do. It simply hasn't had the opportunity to develop, and to allow you to feel comfortable with it.

CONSISTENCY

I mentioned on page 19 that one of the qualities noted by psychologists as a characteristic of psychological maturity is self-knowledge. Another of these qualities is consistency. The psychologically mature person has sufficient integrity of personality to be identifiably him or herself, no matter how difficult or unexpected the context. Psychological immaturity, by contrast, is characterised by a wide diversity of separate 'selves', which lead the individual to operate value systems and to make choices and decisions in one situation that he or she would never dream of making in another. We have of course to wear a different hat in the office from the one we wear at home. And we sometimes vary our approach according to our relationship to different people, and the particular needs they may have. But consistency means that there's an important part of us that is never compromised. Wherever and with whoever we're operating, we're still recognisable as us.

One way of looking at this consistency in ourselves is to go back to the list of adjectives you used in Exercise 2. Would someone who knows you outside work use largely the same words to describe you as someone who knows you on a professional basis? Would a client who knows you well use largely the same words as a neighbour? If not, you may be able to justify the differences to yourself. But they need thinking about.

SELF-CONTROL

In stressing self-knowledge and the need to look at our own behaviour when things go wrong in relationships, I'm not suggesting we're always the ones at fault. But even when the other person is clearly to blame, we shouldn't make the mistake of believing they have a control over our reactions which in fact they don't have.

Let's take an example. We say 'Oh you make me so angry', or 'You make me so nervous', but in reality there are no magic buttons on our chests marked 'anger' or 'nervousness' for other people to press. So in that case how can somebody else *make* me angry or nervous or whatever? The answer of course is that in any direct sense they can't, and that it is *I myself* who makes me react as I do. It's something in me that determines my response, even though it's your behaviour that acts as my cue. If this isn't clear, ask yourself why is it that one individual, with the same remark, may prompt agreement from person A, indifference from person B, and apoplectic rage from person C? The remark doesn't vary. The respective responses are the result of factors within persons A, B and C themselves. Now look at Exercise 3.

INDEPENDENCE AND CONFORMITY

In tackling exercises of this kind, questions often arise as to how much we should conform with others. If the reasons for our difficulties in getting on with someone involve fundamental disagreement with them on major issues, should we give way for the sake of peace, or stand up for what we think to be right?

Research reveals several points about conformity and independence, which contribute of course as much towards our understanding of others as towards our understanding of ourselves.

• Conformers tend to be less sure of themselves, more rigid, more authoritarian in their beliefs, more concerned with what others think, and to have lower self-esteem than non-conformers.

• Non-conformers tend to be more individualistic, more creative, more self-confident, more objective and more able to live with uncertainty ('tolerate ambiguity') than conformers.

• *But* some people deliberately use non-conformity as a way of gaining attention and/or power, either by obstructing group decisions (for example in committee meetings) or by causing shock, amusement or confusion.

Research shows that the people who are respected most do not compromise over their fundamental values or personality traits (back once

EXERCISE 3

Select someone in your life (more than one person if you wish) who prompts negative emotions in you. Write down his or her name and the emotion he or she prompts. Now write a sentence or two, saying what it is in *you* that gives rise to your negative response. Be as objective as you can. Imagine you're talking about someone other than yourself, but who you know very well.

Now select someone in your professional life in whom *you* seem to arouse negative emotions. Write down what it is in you which may be irritating or upsetting them. Yes I know I've just said no one has magic buttons which other people press in order to produce emotional responses. But if we're cueing these responses in others, we need to know why.

When you've identified what it is in you that may be alienating your colleague, decide whether your own behaviour is justified and whether it's the other person who is overreacting. If they are, is there anything you can do to help them cope? Maybe temperamentally they find it hard to find balance in their emotional life. Does it look as if their behaviour brings them much satisfaction? Being human, they'd probably much prefer to get on well with everyone if they could. So maybe they're worth some sympathy, a point to which I return in the next chapter by looking more closely at the need to understand others and the reasons for their behaviour.

If it *doesn't* look as if it's the other person's reactions that are primarily to blame, look once more at the adjectives in Exercise 2. Does one of these have something to tell you about what may be going wrong?

more to our earlier discussion of consistency), but nevertheless have the ability to be flexible where necessary and to be sensitive to the needs of others.

Agreers and disagreers. Allied to conformity and non-conformity is the topic of agreement. Like a reflex action, some people agree with every-thing we say, while others disagree. There is evidence that compulsive agreers – as opposed to people who are simply trying to ingratiate themselves – are low in self-esteem (and need to be encouraged to believe more in themselves). Compulsive disagreers enjoy conflict, have unrealistic self-appraisals (for example they overestimate their own knowledge and abilities), and focus during social exchanges upon their own views rather than upon the quality of argument advanced by the other person.

Compromise. Another allied issue is compromise, an essential feature of social living. Provided it does not go against deeply held beliefs, the ability to compromise (and to identify compromises acceptable to others) wins respect and is an important quality in a good chairperson or leader. If the word 'compromise' sounds suspect, replace it with 'consensus'. They usually amount to the same thing. People willing to compromise tend to be realistic and concerned for the rights of others.

In this chapter we've been looking at ourselves and at some of the ways in which we can improve our professional relationships. However I don't want to give the impression that our social skills within these relationships can or should be reduced to a set of objective responses. We've a right to some of the personal idiosyncracies we use in feeling drawn or otherwise to people. But it's important when there are prob-lems to be able to tease out the identifiable reasons. If they lie in us, and if we decide we want nevertheless to hang on to the behaviour causing them, fine. But at least we now know the price we're paying, and can't reasonably expect other people to pay it for us.

Chapter Three

How Well Do You Know Those You Work With?

The first step in improving our professional social skills, as explored in the last chapter, is to look at ourselves and see what's happening on our side of the relationship. The second, referred to briefly in the last chapter, is to develop a greater understanding of others.

UNDERSTANDING OTHERS

In idle (or stressful!) moments it is nice to wish we could rearrange the world so that it would always perfectly suit our needs, and would be filled with people who possess all the qualities that make our lives convenient and comfortable. But life isn't like that, and the world would probably turn out to be a very dull place if it were. No, we're stuck with other people as they are, and if we want to get on with them we have to learn how to understand and appreciate them for what they are. Exercise 4 will help you do this. It involves thinking of one person at work with whom you find it difficult to get on, and trying to identify some of the things in his or her background that contribute towards their being the person they are.

RELATING TO STUDENTS: SANDRA AND GRANT

☐ *When Exercise 4 was given to a group of primary school teachers on an in-service training course, Sandra focused upon one of the children in her class, Grant. Grant was 10 years old and had been causing her problems all year. He was disruptive, slow-learning, insolent, and often aggressive towards the other children in the class, and she confessed herself frequently at her wits' end to know how to deal with him. However, when she came to write down some short*

UNDERSTANDING OTHERS

Select one person reasonably well-known to you with whom you find it difficult to relate. A senior or junior colleague perhaps, or a student, patient or client. Reflect on their background. What do you know about them and about their lives? If you know next to nothing, decide on ways in which in future you think you will be able to get at some of the necessary information.

What do you know of their emotions and of the circumstances in which they express them? What do you know about their needs? About the things that worry or disturb them? About their disappointments and frustrations at work and possibly at home? Are they facing situations that would cause most of us problems, such as being passed over for promotion perhaps, or receiving little recognition for their efforts and abilities?

If you're in one of the caring professions and the person you've selected is a client who seems incapable of helping themselves or of appreciating your efforts, how much do you know from firsthand experience of what it's like to live their lives? Perhaps they were brought up in a very deprived environment with constant social strife and abuse. Once again, try to identify factors in this environment that may have contributed to make them what they are, and compare these factors with your own environment and with the advantages you've had.

Now write down as many short statements relating to the person concerned as you can.

statements she surprised herself by the number of things she knew about him, once she tried to think of him objectively.

— Grant is brought up by someone he knows as his aunt. She may or may not be his mother. He has no knowledge of his father.

— The rumour is that Grant's 'aunt' has a succession of live-in boyfriends, some of whom are known to be violent.

— Grant lives in a block of municipal flats known to house many problem families.

— Grant suffers from bronchial infections, and is frequently off school.

— He has no friends in class; the other boys dislike him. He's spiteful towards the girls and they avoid him.

— He's always behind with his work. (Why do I never make an opportunity to give him good marks?)

— Grant sometimes comes to school with money. He says he earns it doing odd jobs, but I think he steals it (or am I just prejudiced?).

— I frequently keep Grant in at break (this doesn't do much for his chances of making friends with the other children!).

— Grant has been helpful on the few occasions I've given him jobs to do, though he needs supervision.

— Grant is deceitful, unpredictable, aggressive, sniffling, unlovable and most of the time a flaming nuisance (I'd probably be even worse if I'd been brought up like him). But he's also vulnerable, confused and unhappy. He has a nice smile and sometimes brings me touching little gifts (which I suspect he's stolen – there I go again with my prejudices).

When she discussed her list, Sandra was dismayed she hadn't done more for Grant. Part of the problem was that he made her professional life so difficult it was hard for her to feel much sympathy for him. But when she looked at his situation dispassionately, it was plain to Sandra that there were several things she could do to help him. In particular she could:

1. Stop blaming Grant for being Grant. Obviously he isn't responsible for most of his shortcomings.

2. Try to contact his social worker, and learn more details of his life.

3. Do more to help him catch up with his work when he misses school through his bronchial troubles.

4. Make opportunities to give him good marks for his work, and to praise him in front of the rest of the class.

5. *Stop keeping him in at break, give him more chance to mix with the rest of the class, talk to some of the other boys about letting him join their games.*

6. *Give him more opportunities to help with jobs around the classroom, and encourage him in his efforts. (While he's doing these jobs take the opportunity to have private words with him and get to know him better and thus set up a more friendly relationship.)*

Sandra is realistic enough to know that these changes in her behaviour won't transform her relationship with Grant overnight. But she's convinced they're an important step, and she reported some weeks later that things are now significantly better in class. Grant is responding to the fact that she's now taking more interest in him, and his schoolwork is improving, while he's increasingly co-operative and eager to help. Sandra's interest and friendly attention give him more status in the eyes of the rest of the class, and he's becoming more popular with the other children, and less aggressive towards them.

Sandra realises that because of his neglect at home Grant is in desperate need of attention. Since he doesn't know how to behave well, he's been winning this attention by being difficult. She herself has been making matters worse by taking notice of Grant only when he was being bad. *Now she's making opportunities for giving him attention for being* good. *This encourages him to behave well by showing him that he can get attention by other means than disruption and aggression.*

Most revealingly of all, Sandra confesses that her changed attitude towards Grant makes it easier for her to put up with him without feeling so annoyed. Understanding him better means that she can excuse in her own mind some of the things he does. 'I keep telling myself that there, but for the grace of God, go I and all the rest of us.' Although she doesn't feel that she deserves much credit, Sandra admits it's nice to feel she's now probably treating Grant with more kindness than he's received from anyone else in his life.

Sandra's case shows how, by failing to take the trouble to understand another person, we end up making our own lives more difficult as well as theirs. Sandra is a caring, sensitive person but her battles with Grant had left her concentrating exclusively upon *her* problem rather than upon his. Instead of focusing upon why Grant was as he was, she had focused upon her own feelings of resentment and anger towards him. By failing to help Grant, she had failed to help herself. Once she took the time to identify ways of giving the help he needed, she discovered she also made her own life easier.

RELATING TO SENIOR COLLEAGUES

Sandra's problem involved her relationship with someone who was pro-fessionally dependent on her (this is categorised on page 12 as a Level 5 relationship). But problems occur equally frequently with people who are actually senior to us at work (Level 4). It comes as a surprise to some that the root of these difficulties may lie less with our own insecurity and perceived inadequacies than with those of our seniors. If someone has achieved status, professional success and responsibilities, we tend to think of them as having no reason to feel unsure of themselves, or to need further prestige and recognition. Yet they may be bowed down by the demands made upon them. They may feel inadequate at dealing with these demands, trapped in a job which they dislike but from which they can see no escape. Or they may be frustrated by lack of resources, by staff turnover, by the vagaries of politicians, by the attention of the media. Instead of sharing their worries with junior colleagues, they may forget all social skills and simply vent their inadequacies and frustrations upon them, causing relationship problems which could have been avoided but which they haven't the expertise to handle.

Alternatively, like the rest of us, senior colleagues may have personal problems that sometimes interfere with their professional life. Or they may have personality problems which make them depend too much upon the heady feelings of power and importance. Behind a front of professional competence and personal maturity, they may hide an immature ego that can only be fed by the constant reassurance of its power to dominate the behaviour and the emotions of those below them.

Understanding these things may help us to feel rather less angry or upset when Level 4 relationships prove particularly difficult. There may be little or nothing we can do or say directly to the person causing our problems. Our job opportunities, our promotion, even our careers may lie in their hands. The only remedy may be to try working on ourselves in the light of this understanding, reassuring ourselves that it's less our professional competence or our personal qualities that lie at the centre of the problem than the professional worries or the personal failings of the man or woman with whom we have to deal.

If you do feel it's appropriate (or that you're driven) to take matters up with him or her, requesting an interview, which will give you time to prepare your case, is usually more effective than complaining in the heat of the moment. Think carefully what you want to say. Keep emotions out of it as much as possible (not because they're unimportant but because they're difficult to explain accurately) and stick to simple facts. Recognise the difficulties the boss may be under and try if possible to relate the difficulties you're having to the *job* rather than to the *boss* him or herself. Keep things as impersonal as you can consistent with accuracy. Don't be humble or unnecessarily apologetic, but don't be too confrontational either. People can become very defensive (and thus sometimes very aggressive) if they think they're under personal attack. Especially if the boss has a particularly fragile ego, direct personal criticism may make matters worse rather than better. But if this criticism is necessary, keep it as non-threatening and as unemotional as possible. And in all things be brief. Come quickly to your points, restrict them to the most important and pressing ones, and show that you can keep your head and temper in a crisis.

OTHER PEOPLE'S MOTIVES

If we return a moment to Sandra's case study, we can see that Sandra misunderstood Grant's motives when she interpreted his bad behaviour as a vendetta directed specifically at her. A closer look at his background convinced her this was simplistic. Grant had had no chance to learn how to relate to others and his antisocial behaviour was a sign of his confusion and inadequacy.

We all run the risk of finding ourselves in a position similar to Sandra's. If a relationship is going badly, we tend to think the other person is being deliberately awkward, and probably enjoying it into the bargain. Or if someone makes a rather ambiguous remark to us we fancy we detect hostile undertones. Or if someone neglects to thank us when thanks are called for we conclude they're either insensitive or don't appreciate our help. Or if our colleagues chuckle at our mistakes we assume they've no respect for us.

Part of the problem of course is our natural self-preoccupation. We think much of what goes on in the world out there is directed at us, when in fact most other people are just as centred upon their own affairs as we are upon ours. Admittedly there are times when others deliberately behave badly towards us, but even when people are rude or offhand there's a good chance their intention is much less personal than we think, and that they may even be unaware of the bad impression they're creating. Since some people are much more thick-skinned than others, it's also possible that if someone said to them the things they're saying to us they wouldn't find them in the least offensive. So in fact they have no real conception of the extent to which we may be hurt by them.

A valuable exercise to counteract this tendency towards self-preoccupation is to go through a whole day without attributing motives to others. People who try this exercise are usually intrigued at how much easier life becomes as a result. Instead of mulling over in their minds the things others say to them (and often building up resentment in the process) they find themselves free to turn from one social encounter to another without accumulating useless emotional baggage from each. Life, they report, becomes lighter and – as some put it – more 'playful'. Far from making them less socially effective, people find the exercise improves their efficiency. They recognise that many of the motives they've been attributing to people are probably wrong anyway, and that endless speculation about them doesn't contribute a great deal to the way in which they handle their relationships.

JUDGING PEOPLE

Of course, we can't always avoid attributing motives to people. Sometimes it is essential to recognise what lies behind their behaviour. But at each of the five relationship levels listed on page 11, we're more likely to be accurate in any attribution of motives if we're good judges of others. Most of us like to think the term 'good judge' applies to us (despite much experience to the contrary!). In particular those at management level like to pride themselves on being able to sum others up accurately, and many a promising career has been blighted as a result. But what makes a person a good judge of others? It would be nice to say a degree in psychology, but unfortunately this isn't necessarily true. Over and above academic knowledge or even extensive experience, an essential factor seems to be the ability to concentrate closely upon others – the ability in short to pay close social attention.

In some cases such a skill may come from a desire to use and manipulate others (regrettably some social manipulators are very good judges of their victims), but more often it's the result of sensitivity towards others plus a healthy curiosity. This sensitivity allows one to pick up small clues about people that many would miss. If we're concentrating too much upon ourselves and upon what we want to say next, then not only are we not listening properly to the other person, we are not watching them and may miss telling clues of gesture, facial expression, and body posture.

At their simplest level, these clues tell us how involved the other person is in what they're saying, whether they're listening to us when we're talking, if they agree with us, if they're interested, if they're tense or relaxed, and – perhaps most important of all – if they feel the time has come to break off the conversation. We've all had ample experience of talking to people who miss all *our* social signals, and drone relentlessly on while we edge doorwards, but are we all equally experienced in responding to the social signals of others? The answer isn't always as clear cut as it looks.

SOCIAL SIGNALS

If we're alert to them, the majority of social signals, particularly at the more formal level, are not difficult to identify. Examples of social signals which suggest the listener is bored, pressured for time or nervous include such things as fidgeting, distracted or unfocused attention, exaggerated sighs, glances at a watch or towards the door, half rising from a chair, angry looks, sharp intakes and exhalations of breath, eyes cast upwards, nervous movements of hands and body, nervous clearing of the throat, tension of manner and posture, repeated attempts to break into the conversation.

These may well be supplemented by (often half-finished) statements such as 'Well I really must be . . .', 'Okay then, can we talk about that next time we . . .?', 'It's a pity I haven't time to . . .'. Positive social signals indicating interest and involvement are more direct, and include an alert expression, eye contact, leaning forward, animated conversation and smiles, unforced laughter, and encouraging nods and gestures. (Further instances are given in the section on non-verbal signals on page 55.)

These examples seem obvious enough, yet many people nevertheless remain insensitive to them. Boring somebody or prolonging a social encounter beyond its span of usefulness is highly uneconomic of everyone's time. It may even be actively counterproductive, in that we compel the person to whom we're talking to switch off completely, and thus risk missing vital information. We also make him or her much less anxious to meet us again in the future, and thus we threaten the good relationship we are trying to create.

One of the most culpable forms of insensitive behaviour is that exercised with a captive audience, for example when a senior colleague talks to a junior one. The junior colleague may have no formula for breaking off the meeting without offence, yet he or she may be under much greater time pressures, and may have very good professional reasons for wanting to terminate things and get back to work. Sometimes this situation represents a subtle exercise of power by the senior over the junior. The senior recognises very well that the conversation has gone on too long, yet the unspoken attitude is 'you'll go when I let you go, and not before'.

The same can of course be true when a social worker is interviewing a client, or in any other encounter between a professional and a member of the public (or between an adult and a child). Because we're there to help the client, patient or student, we feel that it is we who are giving up our time, and therefore we who should decide when the interview should start and finish. Yet the other person may have other commitments, or may simply find the interview so much of a strain that they want it over with as soon as possible. Prolonging the interview unnecessarily not only serves to emphasise their inferior position, it does not allow them to give us proper attention or co-operation. In the end they may say or agree to anything just to get out of our office or to get us out of their house.

ESTABLISHING THE FACTS

Of course there is more to being a good judge than attentiveness to social signals. Good judges are also people who know when they need to delay judgements until they have got more detailed information. It is too easy to make snap decisions about people on the basis of their physical appearance or of their faces or their manner of speaking. And yet people who are reticent, even cold on first acquaintance, may often reveal themselves as communicative and warm when we get to know them better. People who put on a convincing show of friendliness (or efficiency, enthusiasm, humour, honesty or whatever) at a first meeting may be quite unable to keep up the act over a longer period of time (as many interviewers who have selected the wrong person for a particular job know to their cost). People who are casual and informal in one context may turn out to be highly structured and formal in another; people who appear vague and ineffectual may turn out to be focused and effective. And so on.

Similarly, useful as listening to other people's impressions of someone may be, it is worth remembering that their reactions are inevitably coloured by their own subjectivity, just as the relationship between them is coloured by both of the personalities involved and not just by one. The rule must be to delay judgement until one has had time and opportunity to come to know the person concerned better for oneself.

The things that a good judge looks for depend upon the *reasons* why he or she is interacting with another person. These vary according to whether the context is social or professional. And within a professional context there are variations according to whether the meeting is between a manager and job applicant, between colleagues, or between professional and client. But, depending upon individual circumstances, a good judge will generally look for clues to the following:

? What is this person offering me and what can I offer them?
? Does their manner suggest confidence or diffidence?
? How well do they cope intellectually with ideas and information?

? Are they open or closed in their thinking?
? Are they able to express, accept and handle feelings?
? Can they relate successfully to others?

Notice here the careful concentration upon the other person. The question 'what do they think of *me*?' can wait until later. Notice also the precision of the language. There are no vague generalisations such as 'do I like him or her?'. Liking is of great importance (though occasionally the attributes needed for a particular post may not be ones to which an employer warms personally), but it arises as a personal response to the kind of specific qualities on the list, and in that sense is dependent upon them.

If the judging involves job interviewing (of which more in the next section), there will of course be specific qualities related to the job that will also come under scrutiny.

A CASE STUDY IN RECRUITMENT

A useful illustration of the need for good judgement when assessing others comes from the problems that recently faced a manufacturing company. Although established for some years, the company's major expansion has taken place over the last decade with the advent of an exceptionally ambitious and able management team. During the last two years, however, they had become aware of some worrying mistakes both in quality control and in the marketing and delivery departments, and of some important lost orders which threatened to interfere with future development plans.

An outside consultant was therefore called in to appraise these departments thoroughly, and she traced the problems to widespread failures by staff to observe specified procedures. A lack of staff initiatives to rectify difficulties as they arose was also noticed, as was an absence of company loyalty and a reluctance to take on responsibilities as required.

Instead of blaming the staff concerned, the management was persuaded by the consultant to look first at their own practices, in particular at their procedures for making appointments at junior or trainee management levels, procedures which are closely linked to what has just been said about good judgement.

At first the management was reluctant to accept that something was wrong with the way in which they made their appointments. But they were helped to see that if people were unable to do their jobs properly, then the fault could well lie in the fact that the wrong people had been selected in the first place. The recruitment procedures were therefore looked at in close detail, and it was found that although the management was meticulous in drawing up detailed and accurate job descriptions before they began interviewing applicants, they had little idea on how to recognise whether candidates had the personal qualities demanded by these descriptions.

The consultant sat in on a sample of these interviews, and identified what was going wrong. In spite of the fact that when approached separately each manager rated him or herself as either a 'good' or a 'very good' judge of people, in reality little or no real judgement was being exercised at all. The consultant drew up a list of the most elementary mistakes that interviewers were making. Here are some examples. The interviewers were:

- failing to put candidates at ease on arrival,
- failing to structure the interview with a proper sequence involving:
  (a) informal ice-breaking questions
  (b) formal questions designed to elicite personal information
  (c) formal questions designed to probe job qualifications
  (d) invitations designed to allow the candidate ask his or her own questions;
- allowing frequent interruptions by secretaries and incoming telephone calls;
- uneven in their demands, asking some candidates much more difficult questions than others;
- asking leading questions;
- monopolising too much of the interview with their own talk, and interrupting the candidate too often;
- introducing irrelevancies such as personal reminiscences;
- signalling boredom;
- failing to listen to the candidate and failing to answer his or her questions;
- neglecting to keep proper records.

The consultant carried out her own assessment of each candidate and found that her ratings rarely agreed with the interviewers' final assessments and resulting appointments. Because of their poor judgement and weak interviewing skills the management made the appointments they deserved, and much of the blame for what was currently going wrong in the company therefore lay with them.

Acknowledging the implications of their mistakes, the management have since restructured their recruitment procedures with the consultant's help, taking into account her criticisms and general recommendations. The result is the compilation of a detailed code of practice for interviewers, and the use of mock interviews under the guidance of the consultant as a way of providing practical training in interviewing skills. Every genuine interview is now video-recorded, and studied afterwards by other members of the team for comment and appraisal. For a more detailed discussion of this area see *Interviewing* by Glynis Breakwell (The British Psychological Society and Routledge, 1990). The company is now looking closely at all other aspects of social skills from the shop floor to the boardroom. Early indications are that this is leading to an increase in efficiency, productivity and job satisfaction all round.

OTHER PEOPLE'S NEEDS

The good manager, the good teacher, the good social worker is the person who can recognise and satisfy needs in others. In return, they receive maximum co-operation and loyalty from workforce, children, clients or whoever. Some needs are highly personal, but many are sufficiently general to be readily identified. For most people they include such things as the need for:

▶ *appreciation* – the recognition and valuation by others of our efforts and abilities;
▶ *significance* – closely related to appreciation, this is the sense that we matter as people;
▶ *power* – related to significance, people need the power to affect decision making in key areas of their lives;
▶ *usefulness* – related to significance, individuals need skills and abilities that are of use to the community;
▶ *acceptance* – acceptance by others of who and what we are, rather than constant criticism;
▶ *understanding* – sympathy and understanding from others concerning our problems;
▶ *direction* – clear guidance when we require it;
▶ *space* – a necessary minimum of personal freedom and privacy;
▶ *leisure* – free time and the relaxation that goes with it;
▶ *companionship* – friends and acquaintances with whom we can talk and share interests;
▶ *stimulation* – an element of variety and distraction in our lives;
▶ *progress* – a sense of advance and achievement, or of working towards some identifiable goal;
▶ *coherence and pattern* – some consistency, structure and meaning in life;
▶ *happiness* – positive emotions and a sense of being in harmony with ourselves and the world.

The ability to relate well to others includes helping them to satisfy at least some of the needs outlined above. In a professional relationship the way we go about this will be different from the way we go about it in a personal one. And in a professional relationship the extent to which we should – or will be able to – help people at the five different Levels (see page 11) will also vary. But in all contexts much depends upon our ability to encourage people to recognise and state their needs. We can't promise in advance to answer these needs, but the very fact of one person articulating them and another person listening to them puts a relationship on a potentially more productive footing.

Once other people's needs have been identified and acknowledged, dialogue alone may not be the best way to satisfy them. For example children, socially inadequate people, people struggling with physical disability or recovering from physical illness clearly need reassurance and encouragement if they are to gain or recover the confidence necessary to meet others on an equal footing. But this reassurance and encouragement should be offered not just through what we tell them about themselves (important as this is), but from what we prompt them to do. Permanent changes in behaviour come not so much from helping people change their attitudes and beliefs by talking to them, but from giving them chances to exercise new behaviour within the context of success.

GIVING AND RECEIVING HELP

One way of creating such chances is to show people that they can play a useful social role. As indicated in the list of needs given above, we like to feel recognised and valued and thus *appreciated*, but we also like to feel *significant* and (to a greater or lesser degree) *powerful*. So we like to receive help, but we also like to give it. Some individuals in fact are almost incapable of accepting help unless they are allowed to give something back in return, even if only at a token level. This enables them to keep a feeling of independence, and is invaluable for their self-esteem. Finding a way of enabling them to do this and thus demonstrate their *usefulness* is one of the arts of the good manager or any good professional.

Research studies show that part of this art often involves asking for help *before* offering it. In this context (or indeed whenever you're requesting help) you're more likely to get it if you ask for something specific ('Can you help me with *this* please?' rather than 'I wonder if I could ask for your help?' or 'I wonder if you would do me a favour?'). Not surprisingly, there's also evidence that if your request for help is a major one it is more likely to be successful if the person you're asking has already helped you over a smaller matter (and received proper appreciation for so doing). The moral therefore is start with a limited request before graduating to a more formidable one!

The kind of help we ask for will depend upon the person to whom we're relating. Social workers and community nurses report that a simple phrase like 'I'm dying for a cup of tea' when they enter a client's house works wonders in getting the encounter off to a good start. Hospital nurses report that asking even quite ill patients to help them in minor matters (like holding a piece of equipment for them during treatment) is similarly effective, especially if it is made clear that this is to help the nurse, not merely to help the patient him or herself. Some nurses cultivate a deliberate awkwardness at times, just to give the patient the opportunity to offer assistance.

At management level, requesting workers for advice and information is an excellent way of helping them feel appreciated. A request (not a demand) of this kind reassures the worker that he or she has expertise that is prized by managers and which the managers themselves do not possess. In fact the good manager often hides his or her knowledge in a particular area, in order to give workers the opportunity to experience this reassurance. The rule is that no matter how simple the advice or the information, if it is at the upper level of the worker's range of expertise, then the latter will feel valued by being given the opportunity to demonstrate it.

Appreciating other people's jokes is another way of showing we value them. Humour is a powerful social force and since we all love laughter, individuals who have the gift of stimulating it naturally feel prized by us. The ability to laugh at ourselves when appropriate is also a help. It shows we are not placing ourselves above others, or using dignity and status as distancing devices, and shows that we accept our fallibility too. The jokes we tell against ourselves needn't be elaborate ones – simply humorous little incidents like losing our way or mislaying our keys or confusing one person with another.

People's needs for *acceptance* and *understanding* can be helped by the listening skills referred to on page 53. The need for *space* presents more difficulties. Psychological space can be respected by not delving unnecessarily deeply into areas of an individual's personal life which they would prefer to keep to themselves, or at the very least allowing them to reveal personal matters in easy stages rather than probing relentlessly for them on the first meeting.

The need for physical space is not so easy. In hospital, for example, many patients find that along with the loss of physical space goes the loss of privacy, and that this is one of the most stressful things they have to face. The same can apply in jobs where individuals have to work close together throughout the day. While social extraverts, who are geared very much towards social interaction and external stimuli, may be able to cope with the experience and find it preferable to solitude, social introverts can find it highly stressful, particularly when there is never any chance of escape.

The only answer is to respect people's need for physical privacy, and find some way, however difficult, of satisfying it. Some hospitals manage this by allowing patients at times to have the screens around them even when they are not undergoing treatment. Some organisations provide a quiet room where staff can go at lunchtimes and during breaks rather than to the canteen. A person who, in ideal circumstances, needs a large room to themselves in order to feel really private will, in unpromising surroundings, often find the same sense of privacy in the corner of a busy room, so long as they know they will be left there in peace.

People's need for *stimulation* and *progress* is in some ways analagous to that for space, in that if they are denied satisfaction of this need in large measure, they will still find a degree of satisfaction if allowed it in small. We all know for example how, when bored, we will turn to almost anything to keep our minds occupied. Similarly with progress, if we can't take big steps forward, we turn our attention to limited ones (as do keen gardeners who inspect their plants every day, alert for and thrilled by each tiny advance). Management who are aware of these factors will find ways of allowing workers both stimulation and progress, no matter how restricted they necessarily have to be in each case.

The best way to discover how stimulation and progress can most usefully be offered is to ask people. This also helps satisfy the need for *power* dealt with earlier, in that people feel they have at least a degree of control over their environment. Stimulation may be provided through the physical environment in the form of particular colours for the walls and paintwork, particular lighting arrangements, and of course background music. In activity terms, it can be provided through short breaks in which workers engage in some brief recreational exercise (as in some Japanese factories), through opportunities for some small variation in the working routine and so on. Progress may take the form of material incentives, of visible marks of seniority, or of perks of one sort or another outside the confines of work itself. But with both stimulation and progress, the essential factor is that a degree of novelty be introduced into working life.

The need for *direction* is served by consistent, unambiguous leadership, which keeps people fully informed of present policy and methodology, as well as future aims and objectives. People vary in the degree of leadership they require. Some prefer the opportunity to exercise initiative; others prefer to be told what to do. But very few people give of their best when faced with weak, inappropriate, opaque and unpredictable leadership. (See page 5 for some of the personal qualities possessed by the good leader.) Poor leadership also fails to satisfy the need for *pattern* which most of us have. Particularly if we are creative we may be able to tolerate a certain degree of ambiguity in our environment, but very few people can function in an atmosphere of chaos, especially when it masquerades under the guise of leadership.

ATTENTION SEEKING

Many of the above needs are bound up with social attention. We may require this attention because we want someone to notice and appreciate what we're doing (for example if we're chasing an important promotion at work), or we may simply need it because it helps us feel significant. If others ignore us, we quickly begin to lose some of our self-confidence and self-esteem. This need for social significance, as mentioned on page 41, is a very powerful factor in human behaviour.

In Level 1 relationships, this need can sometimes take the form of officiousness or obstructiveness as the individuals concerned draw attention to their existence and to the (limited but often inconveniencing) powers which they have over their higher status colleagues. Similarly much bad behaviour in children can be traced to this same bid to be noticed. But people higher up the hierarchy at relationship levels 2–5 may be just as prone to attention-seeking behaviour. Their strategies may be more subtle, for example helplessness at Level 5, dominance at Level 4, competitiveness at Levels 2 and 3, but essentially the motive is the same – to develop and defend a sense of personal significance, whether this be to do with power, importance or whatever.

Generally, if people feel they are being given their due regard, this lessens their need to seek attention. The military practice of sometimes promoting the biggest troublemaker in the platoon to a lance corporal is a useful example of this. Once given a measure of authority, the troublemaker's need for causing trouble disappears. Within organisations, attention seeking is best handled by opening proper channels of promotion and advancement, and also by making sure everyone has a chance to have a say in things that affect their work. As was explained earlier, the latter is especially important, as it recognises the value of each person's judgement, and allows them to have power over their environment and thus, in a sense, their own destiny.

If we go back to the example of Sandra and Grant on page 30, however, we can also see that there are certain kinds of attention-seeking behaviour that are best ignored. Generally, by responding to such behaviour, we strengthen it. Our response shows the individual concerned that attention-seeking behaviour produces results, so he or she is likely to repeat it. Sandra discovered that she should pay more attention to Grant, but that she should be careful to do so in response to *desirable* rather than undesirable behaviour.

Sometimes referred to as *behaviour modification* (though the term smacks far too much of behaviour manipulation for some), research with various groups, from workers to children to psychiatric patients, has shown that ignoring inappropriate attention seeking behaviour wherever possible and responding to appropriate behaviour is a powerful strategy for improving relationships and for helping people change. The strategy works best when we make a systematic inventory of both wanted and unwanted behaviours (specifying each behaviour in some detail – general terms like 'rude and offensive' or 'whining and tearful' are insufficient), and write clearly against each one whether we intend to ignore or respond to it in the future.

If necessary, the specified undesirable behaviours can be arranged in hierarchical order from 'most easily ignored' to 'least easily ignored'. For example, while you cannot ignore the violent behaviour of a client or of a maladjusted child, you can ignore abusive language or routine threats. At the same time you can respond immediately (with friendly conversation, interest, smiles and encouragement) to more civil behaviour and to overtures of friendship. Once you have established a new pattern in your relationship with the client or the child, some of the 'least easily ignored' behaviours may begin to disappear as the person's need for attention begins to decrease.

HELPLESSNESS AND DEPENDENCY

As indicated on page 45, another important form of attention-seeking behaviour involves helplessness and dependency (of action or of thought). People working with or under considerate colleagues, or clients and pupils working with sympathetic professionals, often find ready help when they can't do things for themselves, and may then start to exploit the situation to gain attention. This is particularly likely to happen when confidence or sometimes sheer laziness are involved. People become progressively more dependent upon the helper and less able to show initiative, make decisions and carry through expressed intentions.

Individuals are best served by being helped towards independence, so exploitative attention-seeking of this kind must be discouraged. Ignoring it can sometimes help, but it is preferable to negotiate clear boundaries to the amount of practical help that is going to be given. The best way to do this is through the creation of an informal contract. The helper makes it plain that 'I'm prepared to do this for you, on condition that you are prepared to do that'. As time passes the contract is renegotiated, with increasing emphasis upon the client taking responsibility for him or her self, and attention is always directed towards the things the individual can do rather than towards the things he or she can't. Praise and encouragement are given for every success, no matter how small.

Where simple laziness is also a factor, and where the person being helped lets this prevent them from carrying out their side of the bargain, the most productive strategy is the law of natural consequences. They should be allowed to see that what they don't do doesn't get done, and allowed to experience the results.

SHYNESS

Although people can, of course, act shy to gain other people's attention and concern, shyness usually signals a genuine need for help in relaxing and feeling socially at ease. Few of us are completely free of it (in a recent study only seven per cent of people claimed they never experienced it). It runs right across the ability range, with highly intelligent people no more exempt than slow learners. It runs across the sexes and across age groups and cultural groups. If you watch closely even very outgoing and experienced people, such as media personalities and politicians, you will often notice that under their assured exteriors there are the telltale signs of shyness – the nervous fiddling with spectacles, the sweat on the forehead, the hesitancy and jerkiness of speech.

Most people say their shyness involves trouble in making conversation and in maintaining eye contact, while the physical symptoms involve general discomfort, sweating, excessive body heat, faintness, stumbling over words, and (worst of all) blushing.

Is shyness a natural phenomenon or one we learn? Some small babies certainly show a kind of bashful caution when introduced to strangers, and this caution seems to be the innate potential from which shyness develops. But the nature and strength of its development and the situations which provoke it owe much to learning. This learning stems from experiences, often in childhood and adolescence, when people are on show and open to comment and critical judgement and feel themselves to be wanting. Teasing and unfeeling criticism while they're in the spotlight makes things worse. They become acutely conscious of 'self', and construct an internal representation of the comments and judgements they fancy are being made about them. The incidents concerned spark off inwardly-directed anger and disgust, and nervousness at having to face similar public incidents in the future. Shy people feel they won't be able to handle them, and their feelings become self-fulfilling prophecies. The lesson they learn is that once they're on show they end up looking foolish.

What shy people are experiencing therefore is a form of nervousness, sparked off by feelings of social inadequacy (real or imagined). And the more nervous they are, the more likely actual inadequacy becomes. And the worse the inadequacy, the more self-conscious they are and the more self punitive and awkward they become. And the more self-conscious and self-punitive they become, the worse their nervousness. And so it goes on.

I have something to say in Chapter 5 on how to overcome shyness. But as nearly all of us experience the emotion at some points in our lives, we should have no difficulty in empathising with anyone actively handicapped by it. The suffering caused to the individual by excessive shyness is very real, and calls for all the understanding and help we can offer.

Chapter Four

Effective Communication

THE ESSENTIALS

BEING A GOOD TALKER

The world is full of good talkers. But it isn't that full of *good* talkers. In professional life it is sometimes necessary to talk formally and very much to the point. At other times it is enough to be at social ease with others, whether they be clients, superiors, colleagues, juniors, guests or whoever. One key to being a good talker at each of the five relationship levels is the ability to amuse others. Another is the good sense not to monopolise the conversation. However successful a talker you are, other people want to have their say too. Three other keys are mentioned in the context of helping others to talk purposefully (page 53), namely stay focused, identify the real problems (if any) under discussion, and don't rush in with solutions (at the expense of allowing others to have their say).

A further vital key is of course interest. If we interest the person or persons to whom we're talking, they'll want to listen. Most people demand relevance in a good talker, and this simply means talking about things that clearly relate to their difficulties and to the solutions to these difficulties, or to their interests and to ways of advancing these interests.

We can tell if we're boring people by developing sensitivity to the social signals they send to us (see page 37). The more aware we are of the other person and of their concerns, the less likely we are to bore them. Bores aren't just people who back us into a corner at parties. There are as many bores in professional life as outside it. And the main cause in each case is a faulty awareness of the other person and of the things that matter in his or her life. A secondary cause is inflexibility. I've mentioned the importance of keeping our talking focused rather than rambling and discursive. But this doesn't mean going to the opposite extreme, and refusing to follow new directions in the conversation when these clearly reflect the other person's legitimate and immediate concerns. It also doesn't mean ignoring any questions the other person wants to put. Questions are often an excellent guide to what the other person is really thinking or really interested in or really worried about. To refuse to respond to them is usually to miss a real opportunity of offering help.

Being a good talker also means talking at the right level for our listeners. In professional life we're very often called upon to talk to people who know much less about things than we do, or who are at a much lower level of understanding and of verbal fluency. Without patronising or talking down to them, we have to put things in a form which they can follow. And we have to be aware that no matter how important the matter under discussion is to them, and no matter how good we are at explaining it, they may have a very limited attention span. After a sentence or two their attention wanders, and from there on all our eloquence goes to waste. In these cases it's vital to pause frequently and to check that our listeners are following.

Simple questions such as 'Do you see what I mean?', 'Am I making this clear?' are helpful, but all too often there's a distressing tendency on the part of the listener to answer 'yes' even when we've lost them completely. So a better form of question, like the ones used by good teachers, is to ask for more than a yes or no response. This means asking the listener to give you back a piece of information you've just given them ('So what is it that's so important about . . .?') or to ask them about the implications of what you've just been saying ('So what is this going to mean for you if . . .?').

Another feature of the good talker is an absence of annoying mannerisms of speech or gesture. Constant repetitions of such redundant expressions as 'y'know', 'and so on', 'I mean', and 'right?', can drive even the most patient of listeners to distraction. Almost as infuriating are hands that fiddle incessantly with spectacles or handkerchiefs. If the right facilities are available, it can be a valuable exercise to audio- or video-tape meetings with clients or colleagues, and view one's performance critically afterwards. (If it's any consolation, most people are equally appalled at the results.)

BEING A GOOD LISTENER

The ability to listen is just as important an ingredient of effective communication as the ability to have your say. Good listening implies the ability to take as much interest in the other person's side of the discussion as in your own. If you study closely the behaviour of a colleague to whom you're talking (or maybe your own behaviour when someone is talking to you) you'll see how he or she often can't wait for you to finish what you're saying so they can get in their own contribution. And you'll see how questions they ask you are often simply excuses to start telling you about their own concerns.

BAD LISTENING: SANDRA AND JENNIFER

A piece of dialogue will illustrate this. Sandra is Jennifer's senior colleague in a busy social services department, and knows that Jennifer is having particular difficulties with one of her problem families. She begins to question her on the subject.

SANDRA: *What's happening about that family up on the Greenfield Estate?*

JENNIFER: *Oh you mean the Petersons. Well the big difficulty is that usually there doesn't seem to be anyone at home. I ring the doorbell and . . .*

SANDRA: *Yes I had a family like that. I'm pretty sure they were at home every time I called. But I used to ring and ring and no one came.*

JENNIFER: *Oh I don't think . . .*

SANDRA: *I always used to feel they were watching me through letter boxes or key holes. I used to get quite paranoid about it.*

JENNIFER: *What worries me about the Petersons is that . . .*

SANDRA: *If you worry too much in this job you end up in an early grave. You know Jenny, I always take the view that there's a limit to what we can do. People expect us to be a cross between a saint and a jailor. And yet half the time we're not allowed to be any real use at all.*

JENNIFER: *Oh it's not that I feel useless. My problem is I . . .*

SANDRA: *Let me give you an example of what I mean. I once had a family called the Graingers. She was never out of prison, and he hit the bottle. Each time I went there I . . . .*

And so the conversation goes on, in its maddening one-sided way. Only Jennifer's patience and the fact that she wants to stay on good terms with Sandra prevents her from walking out and finding some better way of spending her time.

Of course, bad listening can take other forms. Some people are adept at switching to automatic pilot and following their own thoughts when others are talking, putting in the 'ohs'?' and 'ahs' and nods and shakes of the head in all the right places. Although less openly preoccupied with themselves and their own doings than the Sandras of this world, they nevertheless take so little interest in the person talking that they prefer their own inner monologue.

Bad listening can also involve continually jumping in and completing whatever it is the other person is trying to say. This can be a sign of impatience, or simply an apparently laudable desire to help a less articulate person say what they mean. The trouble is that in both cases we may well be putting words into his or her mouth. If we really want to hear what the other person is trying to say, then there's no substitute for hearing them out.

Being a good listener does not, of course, mean that we have to sit there and take whatever other people choose to bombard us with. Some people are compulsive talkers and there is no need to always suffer them in silence. But if we don't want to listen, there are ways of holding our ground and of having our say before we allow ourselves to be interrupted, and ways of terminating a conversation firmly but without giving offence. In the above example, Jennifer's problem is that she allows Sandra to dominate her. This is not because she has nothing interesting to say nor because she is inarticulate, but either because her politeness forbids her to keep talking once Sandra butts in, or because she doesn't believe enough in the value of what she is trying to say to insist on saying it.

What Jennifer should do is to continue calmly with what she's saying, without appearing to notice that Sandra has interrupted her. Both will be talking at once, but after a few experiences of this kind Sandra will get the message. If she doesn't, Jennifer should say, politely but very definitely (*not* pleadingly), 'Let me finish'. When faced with compulsive interrupters, it's surprising how few of us choose to be firm in this way. In fact, even the most dominating of television interviewers (prime examples of professional interrupters) will stop talking when treated in this way.

In the longer term, unless her relationship with her senior colleague is particularly difficult, Jennifer should tell Sandra that it is counterproductive to continue to monopolise the conversation. Most compulsive talkers know they talk too much. The best way to help them, whether they be colleagues or clients, is to open the matter up for discussion. If they need to talk so much, why? Do they know the effect it has upon others? Aren't they sufficiently interested in others to want to hear what *they* have to say? A kind of informal contract in which each person agrees to keep silent if the other person feels they're not getting their fair share of the discussion is often a good idea.

QUESTIONING

The art of questioning is vital in forming judgements, in getting to know more about the people with whom we work, and in professional relation-

ACTIVE LISTENING

BOX 4

One doesn't have to be a professional counsellor to help others by listening to them. For example, studies suggest that some patients in psychiatric hospitals improve more quickly if a sympathetic layperson listens to them regularly. Social psychological research suggests that to be a good listener you should pay attention to the following points:

General approach – One of interest, attention and immediacy.

Posture – Body facing the other person, leaning forward with arms and legs uncrossed and with eye contact maintained.

Attitude – Sincere, sympathetic, non-judgemental (a tendency to pass quick judgements can impose our opinion on the other person, can prematurely crystalize issues, or if directed against the other person can discourage them from talking or can make them defensive or aggressive).

Voice – When remarks are made, the voice is lower, softer and slower than usual, and the tone warmer and more thoughtful.

Other aspects of good listening. It helps both parties if the talker can be prompted to talk purposefully. Here are three guidelines towards achieving this:

▶ Keep the talker focused; there's a tendency in many people to wander off the point, particularly if it's a painful one. Prompts such as 'I'd like to hear more about . . .' or 'What was it you were saying about . . .?' or 'It would help me if you gave me more details on . . .' usually guide the talker back to the main issues.

▶ Help the talker identify the real nature of the problem. Often people in trouble are confused about what is *really* wrong. Keeping them focused and asking for more information where necessary helps to produce clarification.

▶ Don't rush in with solutions. These solutions may be fine for you, but inappropriate for the talker. 'What do you think you want to do about it?' is usually much better than 'This is what you must do about it'.

ships in general. Nurses and doctors receive training on questioning within the context of taking medical histories; teachers receive training on how to question in the classroom; and the police receive training on taking evidence. But on the whole, questioning can all too often be something of a hit and miss affair.

One way of thinking about questions is to regard them as 'closed' or 'open'. A closed question invites a simple 'yes', 'no' or 'don't know' answer, while an open question encourages enlargement. In prompting reticent people to talk, open questions are therefore preferable to closed ones. Most closed questions can be translated into open ones; for example 'Did you come here by car?' is a closed question, but 'How did you come here?' is an open one, albeit at a simple level. Simple open questions can usually be translated in turn into more extended ones, for example 'What problems did you have in getting here?'.

It is important not to allow extended questions to turn into portmanteau ones however, with several questions masquerading as one, for example: 'Was there a lot of traffic and was that what held you up and did it make you miss your appointment?' The person on the receiving end of such a question can be nonplussed, and left groping for which part of it to answer.

It is also vital that questions should be pitched at a level the respondent can understand. Words as used by professionals don't always carry the same meaning for other people. So though lay people may appear to understand, they may miss something vital about what is being asked. This can apply to simple words and phrases like 'how long?' or 'often' or 'likely', as well as to technical terms. The moral is, if in doubt, always check whether you're being properly understood. A good way to do this is to rephrase what the other person has just told you ('I see, so what you're saying is . . .'). Another way is to ask for clarification ('Yes, but do you mean that . . .?'). You can also ask for examples ('Could you tell me about the last time that happened?').

Rephrasing questions is also helpful ('Let me put it another way, I wonder if . . .'). It can't be stressed too often that should you fail to receive a proper answer, it may be the fault of the question rather than of the other person. Rephrase several times if necessary. Also be prepared sometimes to ask the *other* person to rephrase for you ('Would you like to put that in your own words?'; 'What do you think I'm really asking you?').

Avoid, of course, leading questions or statements that give indications of your own preferred answers ('I don't suppose you ever do that sort of thing do you?'; 'I hope you're going to tell me it hasn't happened again'). Avoid, too, questions that are beyond the other person's capacity to answer (this applies particularly to the classroom), or questions that are insensitive ('Does your handicap bother you?'), that probe too deeply ('What are your sexual fantasies?') or that are poorly timed ('What are your plans now your husband has died?'). Where possible, make your questioning more precise by deciding whether you want to ask a specification question designed to elicit details or to clarify matters ('Who exactly is it who makes you angry?'; 'Can you give me examples?'), personal reaction questions designed to encourage the expression of thoughts and feelings ('In what way does your work depress you?'; 'How do you react to the thought of leaving home?'), or elaboration questions inviting further examination and expansion ('Can you go more deeply into that feeling?'; 'Tell me more about what happened.').

Finally, remember that the other person should be enabled to see that answering your questions is a way for *them* to help *you*. Rather than adopt an 'If you don't answer my questions I can't help you' approach, aim for one that implies 'It would help clarify things for me if you could tell me . . .'. The first approach interrogates the other person; the second offers a partnership of shared interest and commitment.

NONVERBAL SIGNALS

Professional relationships are principally, but by no means exclusively, expressed through spoken language. There is an extensive literature on nonverbal signals (often referred to as *body language*), which deals with professional and personal issues as diverse as nods and winks on the one hand and sexual contact on the other. The common theme in this literature is that much meaning, from hostility through friendship to the deepest intimacy, can be communicated through these signals, and that we're handicapped in our social skills if we ignore their importance.

Reference was made to body language on page 53 when I discussed the way in which posture can convey whether a person is listening with interest to what someone else is telling them. Body language seems to be a natural part of human social communication, because from the first months of life onwards human beings show visible and often apparently involuntary movements of the facial muscles in response to (and often in harmony with) the person communicating with them. Such *communicative synchrony*, as it is called, plays an important part in maintaining social contact, and it is very disconcerting to talk to someone who stares fixedly at you without moving a facial muscle.

Research with very young children suggests that from early infancy onwards, we reveal an innate tendency to interact physically with the person in front of us. We're social creatures, and we express our social nature through our bodies (by means of posture, gesture and touch) as well as through our words.

TOUCH

Right across cultures, men and women have developed ways to show their acceptance of each other's company through touch. Touch establishes our relationship on meeting and confirms it on parting. A handshake, a hug, a kiss (depending upon the culture and upon the closeness of the relationship) are vital adjuncts to the spoken word, and in some cases far outweigh it in importance.

In professional relationships, touch is less obviously important than it is in personal ones. Nevertheless in professions such as nursing it is part of therapeutic interaction, and here research shows that when sick or in trouble many people feel soothed and comforted simply by the feel of another person's hands upon them.

In non-medical professions, touch can still convey warmth (at greeting and at parting), sympathy and reassurance. But the problem is, when does touch cross over the boundary from professional to personal? In professional relationships, a certain social distance has to be maintained between the parties, and many professionals feel that touch threatens this distance. They worry that it may be misinterpreted by the other person, particularly if he or she is of the opposite sex. Or they feel a personal awkwardness and embarrassment at touching or at being touched.

The safest policy would of course be to restrict touch to no more than a formal handshake. Yet I have seen situations where trained professionals have held back from even placing a comforting hand upon the arm or shoulder of a client in deep distress, and through this remoteness have conveyed unmistakable messages of coldness and disengagement which have undone some of the rapport with the client which they have been at pains to build up.

The suitability or otherwise of professional touch does vary of course from situation to situation, and a golden rule is that no one should ever be made to feel threatened or invaded by such touch. Moreover, except in the case of therapeutic touching (as in nursing), it is best only to touch other people's hands, arms and shoulders. Another rule is that touch which is conveyed artificially and awkwardly instead of spontaneously and naturally is best avoided. It runs the risk of making both parties feel uncomfortable, and can sometimes even diminish rather than enhance a relationship.

SMILING

Finally a word about one of the most important pieces of body language of all, smiling. Research shows that in both personal and professional life people who smile are rated as warm, empathetic and understanding. But the smile must be genuine. A false smile is seen as ingratiating, as submissive, as appeasing, and as associated with artificial or unassertive people. (Some studies suggest a smile that involves the eyes as well as the mouth is rated by most people as more genuine than a smile that involves the mouth only.) The best kind of smile is one that comes spontaneously, from the pleasure of seeing someone. But in professional life people sometimes claim that what holds them back is a fear that smiles weaken their official and competent image. There's no evidence this fear is justified. And most people who try smiling report how much more friendly everyone else suddenly seems to be.

SPECIFIC PROBLEMS

There is a range of specific problems we have to deal with when communicating at a professional level with others. How do we communicate with the shy and socially awkward? How we break bad news, handle confrontations, criticise others perceptively yet sensitively? How do we work with others as a team? Particular difficulties arise when we're dealing with people from other ethnic groups, so let's deal with these first.

OTHER ETHNIC GROUPS

In a multiracial society, the importance of understanding people of varied linguistic and cultural backgrounds, and of making ourselves understood by them, hardly needs stressing. Whether their relationship to us is that of boss or colleague, of worker, or of student or client, our ability to do our best for them and to get the best from them is intimately bound up with the quality of this understanding.

LANGUAGE

Direct experience of working with different ethnic groups (or with foreign nationals resident in the UK) quickly demonstrates the vital part language plays in the way in which individuals project themselves. To be unfamiliar with a language robs people, almost as brutally as physical illness or injury, of much of their personal power. If somebody with little command of English talks to us, they are placed immediately in a role of inequality. Even the simplest instructions seem beyond their comprehension, and even the simplest thoughts beyond their powers of expression. They become potentially a nuisance, a responsibility, a liability, or downright comic, depending on our disposition.

The truth is, rob any man or woman of the ability to communicate fluently through language, and no matter what their intelligence or their ability, they are reduced in many ways to the level of apparent infancy or mental handicap. And the implication of this is that if our roles are reversed and I become the one trying to communicate in the other person's unfamiliar language, then it is they who now become powerful, and it is I who become slow-witted and helpless.

The first moral to arise from this is that we should never assume a lack of intelligence on the part of another simply because they know little English. And the second moral is that they are really a symbol for myself were I placed in their position. Once these morals are absorbed, it becomes easier to be understanding and patient when trying to communicate. To make this communication more efficient, what would I need (and appreciate) if the roles were reversed? First I would need someone to talk to me slowly and distinctly, separating words instead of running them together. Second, I would need them to use simple language. Then third, I would need them to pause frequently to check that I've understood, and to repeat or rephrase things if necessary. And even if I'm apparently fluent in English, I would hope that the other person remembers that although I may *think* I know the meaning of the words being used, misunderstandings can all too frequently arise simply because we both assume I understand when in fact I don't. Similarly, although I may appear rude and abrupt at times when I'm speaking, this is more likely to be because I'm not properly conversant with the niceties of polite speech in their language than because I deliberately mean to offend. Finally, I would hope that they remember that in spite of my problems with language, I would still like to keep my dignity as a mature adult.

CULTURAL DIFFERENCES

What is true of language is also true, in its own way, of cultural differences. Although the other person (to reverse roles again) is living in my culture, he or she may have a set of values, of morals, of social skills which are as valid to him or her as my own are to me, and yet which appear strange, quaint or even at times objectionable to me. I need once more to remind myself that my own values and behaviour may appear equally objectionable to him or her. So long as we both act within the law, we are both entitled to each other's respect. By failing to extend this respect, we may deeply and needlessly offend each other.

Cultural differences extend of course not just to behaviour but also to personality. Much of our personality is determined for us by our environment. The other person may have grown up in an environment in which exuberance, noise, and social extraversion are prized. I may have grown up in one which prizes restraint, calm and social introversion. For me to see him or her as a deliberate nuisance, and for them to see me as deliberately unsociable, would be for each of us sadly to misread the case. In the same way, our social attitudes may be very different. He or she may have suffered racial prejudice or abuse, but to identify me with the abusers simply because I come from the same ethnic group would be as unhelpful as it would be for me to fail to recognise the painful wounds for which this prejudice and abuse are responsible.

Relating well to people from other ethnic groups therefore requires understanding, patience, explanation of our own professional role, and the imaginative ability to put ourselves in their shoes. We also need to respect and appreciate just how deep some of these cultural and linguistic differences lie. So that although the other person may speak even better English than we do, and to all intents and purposes appear even more ethnically British, this should not trick us into thinking we need no longer have regard for these differences. Mistakes of this kind may still lead us to offend when we have no intention of offending, or to misunderstand when we have no intention of misunderstanding.

OTHER SOCIAL GROUPS

Much of what has just been said applies equally to relationships with people from social backgrounds different from our own. There may be similar problems over the use of language, and similar problems over different standards and values, over different cultural behaviour and different personality types. The main variation may lie in recognising these differences. Because the other person's mother tongue is English and we share the same ethnic group, I may fail to make proper allowance for the fact that their upbringing may bear little resemblance to my own.

In addition to having learnt quite different sets of values and standards and quite different sets of social skills and personality characteristics, we may see the social institutions which we share in a quite different light. I may have been brought up, for example, to see those in authority – teachers, police, the social services, politicians – as being on my side, while the other person may have been taught to see them as enemies.

Unless I understand this, my attempts at communication are not going to get very far.

Those who work with different social groups – and in particular with the underprivileged – find that once they begin to see the world through their eyes, much apparently antisocial behaviour becomes more comprehensible. They see that it carries a logic consistent with the way in which those who are responsible for it have been brought up to see the world. And they recognise that once this is acknowledged they can work to produce any necessary changes in this behaviour from the inside, by speaking a language that is verbally and conceptually com prehensible to the people concerned, rather than trying to relate to them from a distance which can only confuse and antagonise.

SHY PEOPLE

Even professional people can suffer from shyness, and if this is so in your case, the strategies outlined in the next chapter for overcoming shyness will be of use to you too. For the moment, the problem is how to relate to shy people and put them at their ease.

- The first and most obvious point is that as shy people are over-conscious of being on show and of being judged, an unnecessarily critical attitude should be avoided.

- Similarly, it is most helpful to appear not to notice other people's shyness *unless* the circumstances are appropriate for talking about it. Once privacy, sufficient time for adequate discussion and a degree of rapport between the parties concerned all exist, 'I expect you're shy about this . . .' is much better than 'I can see you're shy about this . . .'. Shy people often feel better when their shyness is opened for sympathetic discussion, but they don't like to feel it is too obvious.

- Be welcoming, but not too overpowering. Sit beside the shy person, rather than directly in front, and at the same level rather than above them.

- Occupy yourself with something at the beginning of the interview (making tea, looking for a relevant book on the bookshelves) which takes your attention off the shy person and gives them time to settle and feel more at home.

- Although eye contact is still important, it shouldn't be overdone with shy people; make sure they aren't always the first to look away.

- Give the shy person an early opportunity for social success, for example by giving them a question or two which you know they can answer easily, and the answers to which show them in a favourable light ('I hear you did well at . . .?', or 'How did you manage to handle that so nicely . . .?').

- Be relaxed and at ease yourself; most shy people report that relating to someone else who is awkward and tongue-tied only makes their condition worse.

- Allow the shy person time to talk; don't interrupt or try to be 'helpful' by constantly finishing their sentences for them.

- Avoid confrontation; if this isn't possible, give the person time to feel at their ease before it is introduced, and then don't introduce it too abruptly.

- Try and be informal and low-key, with a 'democratic' rather than an authoritarian approach.

The above points apply not just to shy people, but to putting anyone at their ease in a social encounter. But remember that shy people require that little bit more consideration than normal. In extreme cases shyness can be a crippling social problem, as real in its way as a physical handicap.

STAMMERING AND STUTTERING

Everything that has been said about relating to shy people applies equally to people who stutter or stammer. (Often in fact shyness and one or other of these disabilities go together, with one compounding the other.) In addition there are two helpful pieces of advice you can offer sufferers. Firstly, slow the speech right down. Much stammering and stuttering (and cluttering, where the words tumble over each other and get in each other's way) is dramatically alleviated if the sufferer slows speech into a deliberate, rounded drawl. Secondly, drop the level of the voice (even to a whisper if necessary). Stammering and stuttering become worse as the voice is raised (except in song), and better if it is lowered.

BRINGING PEOPLE INTO THE CONVERSATION

Shy people, strangers, nervous people, those who feel out of their depth, members of one sex in a group dominated by the other, may all find difficulty in joining in group debate or conversation. At a professional level this may happen in teaching groups, therapeutic groups, planning groups or in virtually any group brought together for reasons other than the purely social. Bringing such people into group discussion is an important skill, both because it helps the social development of the people concerned and because they may have a valuable contribution to make.

The wrong way to do this is suddenly to focus group attention upon the hapless individual concerned. The right way is to open up appropriate opportunities in the hope that he or she will make use of them. This can be done by introducing a topic with which they are likely to be familiar, and looking across at them with an enquiring expression. If there isn't a suitable opportunity for this, suggest that each person in turn be given the chance *if they wish* to say a word or two on the subject under debate. If this isn't appropriate, a topic on which you know the person concerned has decided views can be brought up, and a low-key comment offered such as 'I know X has thought a lot about this' (rather than 'X has something to say about this').

If you're the group leader you obviously have particular responsibilities, and where possible it's useful to have a word with the person before the meeting and establish what they would like to say and how they can best be brought into the conversation. Asking everyone to introduce themselves by name at the beginning of the meeting, and saying a word or two of welcome yourself to any strangers, is also a great help.

When the person concerned has had their say, support their comment in some way, with thanks or with a follow-up comment of your own, so that they will be encouraged to speak again at an appropriate moment.

COMMUNICATING SYMPATHY

Let's move next from these issues to a very different area, but one which in its way raises just as many problems. In theory, communicating to someone how sorry we are for their misfortune should not be difficult. We feel our sadness for them, and we ought to be able to express it. Why then do we so often find ourselves confessing afterwards 'I just didn't know what to say'?

Sometimes it is because, faced by another's heartbreak, we have a feeling of complete helplessness. In the presence of their bereavement, or ill-health, or agony over the break-up of an intimate personal relationship, words seem to lose their meaning. The only reality in that moment is the other person's distress, and the empathy within ourselves that can prompt us to feel that distress almost as if it were our own. On these occasions in fact, words may take second place to physical contact. If the professional relationship allows it, a hug or a holding of hands may be the best thing we have immediately to offer, and this close contact may also ease our own feelings of impotence. At least we're conveying *something* to the other person, something warm and natural, instead of stumbling over our words or doing nothing at all.

But the right words also have their place, if we can only find them. The first essential is to accept the other person's feelings, instead of attempting to deny them ('Oh surely it can't be as bad as all that') or to reject them ('Oh do pull yourself together!'). Acceptance of feelings should be expressed simply and directly, for example by an invitation to 'Just let go of them' (much better than 'I know how you feel', which invites the bitter response 'You *don't*, you *can't*!'). If the process of letting go is especially painful, an attempt to talk while it's happening is often misplaced. But afterwards, there are some valuable guidelines to bear in mind.

First, grief is a necessary process, and takes time to work through. It is wrong to try to short-circuit it. But at the onset of grief a person often feels lost and helpless, as if the process will go on for eternity, so that there is nothing left to live for. It can be a comfort to tell them gently that with time, the pain will become a little less, hard as it is to believe this now. Second, if the grief is caused by bereavement, people are best helped if you show personal sadness over the loss of their loved one, rather than simply sympathy with them over their loss. The first response confirms the rightness of their grief, indicates in a practical way that you feel something of what they're feeling because you also mourn, and helps to give them a sense of a sadness shared. The second response often makes people feel worse and sometimes even guilty ('Why are they sympathising with me when it is X who has died?').

Even if you didn't know the person who is the cause of the grief, it is still better to focus upon him or her, rather than exclusively upon offering sympathy for the feelings of the one who has been bereaved. Inviting the latter to talk about him or her, and commenting that 'I can see why everyone misses X so much' is an appropriate way of doing this. It may prompt further tears, but both it and the tears are an important part of the healing process.

Third, people are helped to feel less alone if they know you have had a similar experience in your own life and come through it. Fourth, if appropriate, they're helped if you offer practical assistance in planning their future and coping with their problems. And fifth, people need to know they will continue to receive your support, so a firm commitment to come and see them again at a stated time is the best way to part.

BREAKING BAD NEWS

A closely related topic is communicating bad news. Nurses, doctors and the police find this an especially harrowing part of their work, but managers can also come up against the problem, for example when there are redundancies to announce. There is not and cannot be any easy way of breaking bad news, because however it is handled, the tragedy of the news still remains. But it is vital that a path be found between breaking the news too abruptly, and skirting too much around it. The former makes the shock even more severe; the latter builds up anxiety. The initial step is obviously to see that the person is sitting down. This reduces the risk of fainting, and of physical injury if fainting occurs. The next step is to ensure that your tone of voice is gentle and caring, not brisk and 'professional'. The third step is to use a form of words which prepares the person as much as possible for what is to follow, as in 'I'm very sorry but I'm afraid it's bad news'. Then the news itself should be conveyed simply and directly, making sure that nothing is said (such as references to the great pain or distress of a loved one who has just died) to add to the suffering. Details should be kept to the most relevant, and any questions then answered sensitively and sensibly.

It is worth remembering that the props of normality, such as a cup of tea or coffee, are a great help at this point. It is also crucial to remember that people are shocked and stunned on receiving bad news, and often unable to feel or express their emotions straight away. This may make them appear a little casual, as if they are accepting things more readily than they really are. Or they may respond with an apparently inappropriate emotion, such as laughter or irritation. Or they may be disbelieving, or angry with the bearer of bad news. All of these things must be accepted, and not allowed to interfere with the sympathy and sensitivity which the distressed person so badly needs at this time. With those who are able to show their feelings, the previous section on offering sympathy applies. Should the feelings involve hysteria, or the loss of physical control, then providing it is helpful to the relationship, *holding* (the firm but sensitive embrace which prevents people from damaging themselves, and helps ground them) is the best response.

If there are practical things that need to be done – arrangements to be made, other people to be contacted – assurances must be given that these will be taken care of, so that at least these worries can be set on one side. Finally, after receiving bad news, people should never be left alone. If you are unable to stay with them, then a friend or a neighbour or another professional should remain in your place. Not only does this guard against any risk of self-inflicted injury, it reassures the person of a shared humanity, and of the warmth of human compassion and understanding.

CONFLICT-SEEKERS

Now for a very different issue, conflict. Some people thrive on conflict for its own sake. They are often high sensation-seekers, on the lookout for excitement, change and challenge. Typically, they may feel little real antipathy towards the people with whom they're in conflict. They tend to forget the acrimony the moment it's over; it is of no more significance to them than an invigorating game of tennis or squash. There are other people to whom conflict appeals because it allows them to impose their point of view; they thrive not so much upon the conflict itself as upon dominating others. And to others, the conflict is important only as a means to an end. Their real concern is with the issues involved, and with getting their own way over them.

For those to whom conflict isn't the spice of life, it is important to recognise to which of these three categories the person starting the conflict belongs. If it's the first, the point to bear in mind is that he or she is enjoying the encounter. To them it's a game, and there's no reason why you should take it any more seriously than they do, nor is there any reason why you should enter into the game unless you want to. If you decide against it, tell them you can see they're itching for a fight, but that you're too busy (or just can't be bothered) to join in. If in spite of yourself you become involved, keep your side light-hearted. Show it doesn't really matter that much to you either. Conceding that 'if you want to believe that (or behave like that) it's up to you' is often the best strategy. This is often the end of things, since the point of the exercise for the other person isn't so much to convince you as to enjoy the process of arguing.

However, if you're up against someone who feeds upon the defeat of others, you may feel that it's important to stand your ground. Remind yourself that if you show you're upset, you've given the other person the very thing they want, and made them that much more likely to pick upon you again next time they have the chance. If you can actually keep yourself from being upset, that's better still. There's no easy way to do this, but becoming aware of the emotion as it arises and refusing to identify with it is one strategy. Each time we practise this we become that bit better at doing it, and that much closer to understanding and guiding our own emotional life.

It helps, too, if you're able to take a certain amount of control over the situation. People who don't seek or enjoy conflict usually get little practice at it. They therefore lack the experience of the person confronting them, who may be a near-professional at seeking and handling quarrels, and who is thus in complete charge of the situation from start to finish. Staying calm, if possible, helps. If this isn't possible, at least slow things down. The other person shouldn't be allowed to dictate the tempo. With the adrenalin flowing he or she may be at their best when engaged in quick-fire thinking. Slowing down your speed of reply makes this kind of thinking more difficult for them. If you feel too agitated to do this, physical movement helps. Get up and move around.

And remember, unless there are compelling professional reasons why you shouldn't, if you feel very angry – explode and feel good about it afterwards. People who don't seek conflict tend to be peaceable souls, who feel embarrassed and guilty for any display of temper. If you're in this category, the advice is forget the embarrassment and the guilt. You have as much right to be angry as anyone else. Be positive about your anger.

If you're up against people in the third category, who depend on arguing in order to get their way, the only answer is to be sure of your own facts and confident enough to stand your ground. Such people have a habit of moving the debate into the territory which best suits them. They ask rapid questions over points of detail, and are often adept at shifting any blame onto your shoulders rather than their own. The remedy is to be properly briefed, to have your own points carefully marshalled in readiness in your mind, and not to allow yourself to be sidetracked or to let emotion enter into it.

Of course, not all people who become frequently involved in conflict relish or are good at it in the way that the three categories of people described above are. Some people are unnaturally defensive, and persistently take offence where none is intended. Others seem generally at odds with the world, and can't get on well with anyone. Others are territorial, and resent anyone trespassing into what they consider their area. In these cases, the individual's unfriendly behaviour towards you tells you more about themselves than it does about you. They see the world in a particular way, and interpret everything that happens to them accordingly.

The following general guidelines will help you to handle conflict:

▶ Don't take verbal attacks on you too personally, as the person concerned probably behaves like this to most people.
▶ Adopt a consistent approach towards conflict-prone people, so that at least they know where they stand with you.
▶ Don't be taken by surprise by conflict; know who is likely to confront you and when, and be prepared for them.
▶ Don't be pushed immediately onto the defensive. People who are adept at conflict know how to manoeuvre you into a position where you have to justify your behaviour or apologise for it; then all they have to do is keep finding fault with your excuses.
▶ Instead of going onto the defensive, identify an area of the other person's behaviour and request information about it ('Oh that reminds me, what did you mean when . . ? ').

▶ Set a time limit on the discussion right at the outset – a glance at your watch and 'I can only spare three minutes to talk about this' is usually the best way. Terminate the discussion the moment time is up ('I'm going to have to leave it at that . . . ').

RESPONDING TO GRIEVANCES

Sometimes we're confronted by a person who feels they have a genuine grievance against us. On such occasions, there is much good psychological sense in the old adage about the soft answer turning away wrath. (Perhaps 'non-aggressive' is a better word than 'soft'.) In human relationships, all too often aggression begets aggression.

A non-aggressive response, which acknowledges the strength of the other person's feelings before turning to the actual issues involved, lowers the temperature and leaves more room for manoeuvre. In listening to grievances against ourselves, it's all too easy to allow our emotions to surface, and to respond to *them* rather than to the facts of the case and to start phrasing our answer in our own minds instead of listening to what is being said. The most sensible approach is to hear the other person out, avoiding interruptions but (if you're at your desk), making a note or two of what he or she is saying to help you structure your reply.

When the time comes for this reply, concentrate first of all on the facts of the case. Correct any that are inaccurate. Make sure there is some consensus on exactly what the discussion is about before going further. Then, if the grievance is genuine, say a word or two of frank and appropriate apology, and address attention towards how things can be put right. If the grievance is unfair or based upon a misunderstanding of your motives, make this firmly clear. If the other person interrupts, remind him or her that you heard them out, and that you expect them to do the same for you. Don't set out to score debating points or make them look foolish. Even if the other person is obviously in the wrong, it may nevertheless be appropriate to thank them for raising the matter, so that things can be cleared up. Try to close the matter there and then, so that both of you feel it has been given a proper hearing, and that you can part on good terms – 'Okay, we've cleared the air and I think we both understand each other. It's nice to know we can leave it at that.'.

HANDLING CONFRONTATIONS

In handling more formal confrontations, such as those that take place in professional life at committee and other meetings, three simple guidelines are:

Anticipate — Avoid — Answer

Anticipate means thinking ahead and identifying the kinds of confrontation that are likely to occur. Who will be at a particular meeting for example, and what issues will they raise? In what way might you lay yourself open to attack? To misunderstanding? Who is likely to feel threatened by you or your proposals? Who are your friends, and will it help to talk to them before the meeting?

It is a fact of life that when a difficult meeting is in prospect, we tend to shut it out of our thinking as much as possible. With the result that when we arrive at the meeting we're unprepared and less able to handle things successfully. Anticipate doesn't mean dreaming up trouble where none exists. It means taking a realistic view of the prospects, and accepting that when they become reality we'll be kicking ourselves for not paying them more attention.

To *avoid* confrontations doesn't mean running away from them; it means identifying ways of defusing them if they serve no useful purpose. I've already discussed the fact that some people enjoy conflict for its own sake, even though it risks polarising opinions and thus interfering with consensus and decision making. People become forced into opposing camps, and small issues that with goodwill could be settled in minutes become major issues for lengthy accusation, counter-accusation and debate.

Of course if people are determined on conflict, it isn't always possible to avoid. But, the most effective strategy for doing so is to stress positive things (such as the things we can do rather than the things we can't; the areas where we can reach agreement rather than the areas where agreement is impossible). Positive things have a unifying and disarming effect. Of itself this strategy doesn't necessarily yield decisions, but it changes the atmosphere in which those decisions have to be taken, and makes them more likely. And not surprisingly, positive comment from one person often leads to positive comments from someone else.

Another positive approach is to reorientate the meeting. For example, 'Let's get back to the point at issue', or 'It's time someone made a concrete proposal', or even 'There must be a better way of settling things than this'. Comments of this kind only sound sanctimonious if one excludes oneself from them – for example by saying 'If *you* could all stop shouting at each other we could get back to the point' rather than 'If *we* could all stop shouting at each other . . . '.

If, in addition to handling conflict, you have an argument of your own to win, the best strategy is consistently to advance one or two strong reasons in its support. If you advance a long list of them, others will direct their attack at the weakest, thus destroying the credibility of the stronger ones before they even have a chance to figure in the debate.

The third guideline for handling formal confrontations, *answer*, means having an appropriate response if and when the confrontation does occur. The best responses tend to be the ones thought about in advance by individuals perceptive enough to predict the direction the meeting is going to take, or who are very clear as to what they want to emerge from it. By *actors* in other words, rather than by *re-actors*. Often the 'actor' will have something prepared on paper, with copies for everyone (when people have to share copies they pay less attention to them and much of the impact is lost). The 'actor' comes with his or her material marshalled and solutions prepared, while 're-actors' are still groping around for guidance and leadership as things happen.

Although highly-charged emotional answers can be very effective at the right time, they often stop others from taking you too seriously. In the case of a woman, the general response may be sympathy; in the case of a man embarrassment or anger. But either way, the tendency henceforth will be to judge the individual in terms of his or her emotions rather than in terms of his or her arguments, the kiss of death to any sustained hopes of influencing decision making.

Brevity is another excellent quality at a meeting. Points delivered in clear, precise and economical language stand far more chance of impressing colleagues than rambling and tedious ones. It isn't always the case that people are anxious to get the meeting over and done with as quickly as possible. Strange as it may seem, many individuals enjoy prolonging meetings (perhaps so as to delay getting down to 'real' work with a clear conscience?) None the less, they will lose the thread of a long statement, and respond more favourably to one which is clear and precise.

CRITICISING OTHERS

Let's turn now from conflict itself to an issue that often results in conflict, namely criticism. We may be excused for thinking that some people are born critics. The consistent and needless fault-finding indulged in by such people may be a sign of a self-centred and unrealistic approach to life (expecting the world always to be the way they want it), or of an attempt to boost themselves by putting others down, or of a misplaced desire that everyone should operate the same standards that they do. Nevertheless, when sensible and constructive, criticism has an

SELF-EVALUATION

BOX 5

Praise. Some people find it as hard to give or receive praise as others do to criticise. Others can give but not receive, and vice versa. Failure to praise others often reflects a critical attitude to life, or a feeling that to elevate others is somehow to downgrade yourself. Failure to accept praise can reflect fear of flattery, an undue modesty, or embarrassment at being the focus of admiring attention.

The best way to give praise is to forget yourself and concentrate on the performance of the other person. If it's good by their standards, it deserves praise (and the encouragement that goes with praise). The best way to receive praise is to take it kindly but not too seriously – today you may be doing well, tomorrow badly. But where praise is sincerely meant, a simple 'thank you' or 'yes I was pleased about that too' is appropriate. Flattery is best met with a simple statement of fact. 'No, that's no credit of mine'; 'No, that's part of my job'.

Modesty is better than an inflated ego, but if you constantly understate yourself people come to doubt your worth. The rule is: be accurate. Describe yourself in the same fair and open terms you would someone else.

Owning one's own faults. Exaggerated self-criticism is a sign of insecurity, as is a refusal to self-criticise. Genuine self-assertion allows you to recognise and accept your faults, just as you accept them in others. We each have a right not to pretend to be perfect. And owning your faults allows you the insight to work upon them.

important part to play in professional relationships. Not all of us find it an easy thing to offer however.

The ability to criticise, firmly and fairly, depends not only upon an objective knowledge of all the relevant facts and upon a degree of self-conviction, but also upon a certain sensitivity towards the other person. This is often overlooked. For our criticism to be constructive and productive, rather than damaging and counterproductive, we need to realise that some people are much more easily hurt than others, and to recognise that while some people only need a quiet word or two, others require more forceful language. While some people become defensive and hostile if they are criticised too directly, others respond best to plain talking. The main guidelines for effective criticism are:

▶ Keep it constructive – that means helping people see how they can improve, not simply pointing out where they go wrong.

▶ Don't be too personal – criticise the individual's *behaviour* rather than the person him or herself ('You could have handled that better by . . . ' not 'You're too thoughtless to handle that kind of situation').

• Don't antagonise – criticism is counterproductive if it makes people resentful and bitter.

• Help matters by referring to things the person does *well*, not just to the things they do badly ('I was pleased with how you handled A; but with B you could have . . . '). This protects their self-esteem, and leaves them feeling they both want and have the power to improve.

• Keep your criticisms short and to the point, so that the other person is clear what they need to do in future.

• Use moderate language and an efficient but not needlessly stiff and cold manner.

• Let the other person give their side of the story – they'll be more co-operative if they've had a fair hearing.

And part if possible on friendly and optimistic terms, conveying your strong conviction in the other person's ability to make the necessary improvements.

COMMUNICATION AND TEAMWORK

WORKING AS A TEAM

Although the emphasis of the book is upon how you or I, as individuals, can develop our professional social skills, there are often occasions when we're working together with colleagues as a team. Communication and co-operation within the team are vital elements of team success, and studies show that such communication and co-operation work best when:

☐each person is clear as to their role within the team;

☐each person is valued by the team and able to feel that they have something to contribute;

☐each person is seen by the others as pulling their weight;

☐team decisions are democratic and involve a sense of shared responsibility;

☐team members share a similar professional philosophy and similar professional objectives;

☐individual specialisations and approaches within the team complement rather than conflict with each other;

☐individuals are prepared to submerge personal differences in the interests of the team;

☐team norms are sufficiently flexible and open-ended to allow for development and for a creative approach to problem solving.

More general studies also show the need for individuals within the team who can reduce tensions (for example by humour or the ability to propose acceptable forms of compromise), who can help the team develop a sense of identity, and who can provide direction and motivation when necessary. The last three qualities are, together with the other qualities of leadership discussed on page 5, essential attributes of the good team leader.

At an organisational level, the team needs to meet together sufficiently often to develop a sense of unity and shared purpose. On the other hand, it should not meet so often that members come to see these meetings as irrelevant or as interfering with their actual professional duties, and as a result begin to associate them with tedium and time wasting. Meeting socially, even if only over cups of morning coffee, often forges this unity much more surely than irrelevant formal meetings.

TEAM DECISION MAKING

It is vital that crucial team decisions should never be taken without the knowledge and, if possible, the active participation of individual team members. Otherwise, resentment builds up and rapidly destroys the sense of corporate responsibility. People like and need to feel involved, to feel that they have important contributions to make to the decision-making process, especially when decisions directly affect their own work. Since decision making is often such an important part of team functioning, it is also vital that everyone is fully informed of relevant facts, and of the implications of any decisions that are actually taken.

Usually of course the team will have a leader, whether democratically elected or not, whose job it is to act as chairperson, to provide an agenda, and to make sure that these facts and implications are available. The art of chairing meetings cannot easily be summarised in a few lines, but in addition to the duties just mentioned, the chairperson of a team meeting is responsible for ensuring that discussions remain properly focused on the business in hand, that everyone has their say in decision making, that no one is allowed to dominate unreasonably, and that when decisions are taken they are properly understood and democratically accepted by everyone.

When the problem on which the team is trying to reach a decision appears impassable, *brain storming* is sometimes the best way forward. This technique involves inviting people to contribute solutions as they enter their heads, regardless how absurd they seem. Released from the fear that their suggestions may be 'judged' (no matter how diplomatically) by other team members, individuals are able to give full rein to their creativity, often spontaneously producing the germ of a good idea which can then be further developed.

GROUP AND INDIVIDUAL PRESSURES

Although the team can usefully create subgroups, and arrange for individuals who particularly enjoy working together to form pairs or whatever, a team will rapidly lose its cohesion if these subgroups pull in different directions. The good team leader will see to it that matters such as this are opened up for general team debate before attitudes become too hardened. The best approach is to ensure that the team stays focused on larger team goals ('What are our aims as a team?'; 'What are we trying to do as a team?'; 'How can we solve this as a team?'). Over and above this, team members can be helped to see that although there should be no question of incompatible people being forced to work together, nevertheless a certain creative tension between individuals can help them to clarify their own thinking and stimulate and challenge others.

Needless to say, it is axiomatic that no good team easily allows one of its members to become too isolated and unsupported. Such isolation becomes a possibility when one team member is very different in personality or professional outlook from the others. Again it's important that, if possible, this isolation is remedied before it goes too far. The important questions for the team to ask itself are 'Are we doing enough to help X feel one of us? If not, what more can and should we do? Does X feel sufficiently valued? Do we try and draw him or her into our social life? Have they grievances which they feel are unaired? Are they being given fair opportunities within the team? If someone should talk to them individually and find out what's wrong, who is the best person to do this?'

If in spite of everything X prefers to go his or her own way, then in the final analysis there's often little that can be done about it. But if this exit affects team functioning, he or she must at least be helped to see the price that is being paid by others on their behalf.

MULTIDISCIPLINARY TEAMWORK

Finally, professionals often have to communicate with colleagues from other disciplines. Difficulties may arise if technical terms mean different things to the various individuals concerned (as might happen for example if a teacher and a social worker are both discussing school refusal); if the same problem is viewed from areas of quite different professional philosophies and duties (as when a police officer and a psychologist are discussing antisocial behaviour, or a manager and a personnel officer are discussing a worker's personal problems); and when there are apparent differences in professional status (as when a nurse is discussing a patient's treatment with a doctor).

Difficulties over technical terms can be resolved by recognising their existence (all too often they're overlooked right from the start), and by clarification and consensus. But difficulties over professional philosophies and duties, and difficulties over status, are not so easily handled. The former are best addressed by identifying the nature of these difficulties, respecting their right to exist, and attempting as far as possible a complementary approach to the problem under discussion rather than a conflicting one. This can be done by a clear demarcation of responsibilities, an agreement by each individual not to trespass upon the other's area, and a frank acceptance that at times there are bound to be disagreements, but that these are better brought forward for debate rather than allowed to sow the seeds of misunderstanding and antagonism.

Difficulties over professional status are often more to do with professional pride (and insecurity) on both sides than with actual professional issues. With goodwill and mutual respect, they need rarely arise. But the key to their resolution is to put the interests of the third party (in the case of nurses and doctors, the patient) first and personal considerations second. This is easily managed in theory, but in practice it is often thwarted by our ability to delude ourselves that our own interests *are* the third party's interests. When this happens and both parties become deeply entrenched, the arbitration of someone who can take an objective view of events is called for. If there is no formal machinery for this, a colleague who is respected by both sides is the obvious answer. A joint approach should be made to him or her, with both sides then putting their case. Unless tempers run too high, both sides should be present to hear the case of the other, so that they have the opportunity to make comments of fact upon it.

Difficulties over status are best avoided rather than treated. We must of course recognise when we are acting unreasonably ourselves. But it is also appropriate to draw other people's attention to their own behaviour. This is best done on the basis of fact rather than on the basis of emotion. It isn't always easy to be factual and objective when a professional colleague, who should know better, is behaving in a self-centred and (we may think) petty way. But it's worth the effort, because light rather than heat is what is needed. 'Let's look at the issues' is the best approach. At the same time, it's politic (and fair) to protect the professional self-esteem of the other person. Acknowledge their expertise. Respect their professional judgement. Rather than seek obvious 'victory', look for a solution which is really going to serve the best interests of both professions and of any third parties innocently involved.

Chapter Five

Managing Change

One of the major themes underlying this book is that we have the power to change unsatisfactory aspects of the way we relate professionally to others. Through a greater understanding of those with whom we work and of ourselves, we can foster the ability to communicate effectively and rewardingly in our relationships, to the professional and personal benefit of all concerned. In this final chapter, I round off this theme by looking at a number of important general areas where guidance is often needed in helping ourselves and others manage changes in these relationships, and in handling the personal stress that difficulties with these relationships may produce.

OVERCOMING SHYNESS

People suffering from acute shyness can be counselled to find ways of distracting themselves from this extreme consciousness of 'self'. We're never shy if we forget the self, if we forget that we're the doer of a particular action and simply get on and do it. The sharper our ability to concentrate upon one thing (in this case the action) at the expense of another (in this case the actor), the easier it is to achieve this. If there is no obvious action upon which to concentrate, our attention can be focused upon other people, upon what they're saying, how they look, what they're doing.

For people who find this level of concentration beyond them, an alternative strategy is to practise attaching less significance to the feelings of shyness as they occur. As with so many negative emotions, once the feeling of shyness arises individuals tend to invest it with importance. They feel out of control, anxious about being anxious, over-conscious of their burning face and shining forehead. The more they fight against these things, the worse they become. It is therefore more effective to give the blush 'permission' to be there. Paradoxically, once this is done, the blushing will usually decrease.

This technique is similar to what is known as *paradoxical intention*, in which the therapist tells the client to try their hardest to experience *now* whatever unwanted emotion or habit is the focus of treatment. In fact, the harder they try, the harder it is. Paradoxically, the more we try to prevent an emotion, the stronger it often becomes, whereas the more we try to encourage it, the more elusive.

Relaxation and visualisation exercises, as when handling any difficult situation, are also important. Individuals can be helped to put themselves in a relaxed state (see page 82) and then mentally to rehearse in their minds a detailed situation in which they anticipate shyness. They then imagine themselves staying relaxed and cool during the situation itself. If and when the feeling of shyness arises during this exercise, the visualisation can be discontinued and the relaxation restored before the visualisation is re-established.

When doing this exercise, remind people they have no difficulty in walking across a room naturally when they're on their own. Why, objectively, should there be any difference when the room is full of people? The physical movements of walking remain the same. Similarly a person on their own has no difficulty in knowing what to do with their hands or in knowing where to look. Why, objectively, should everything become unnatural just because there are onlookers? People who are shy should concentrate upon being themselves as they normally are, instead of building up an internalised picture of themselves as a gauche object in other people's landscapes.

Another strategy is to counsel individuals to look at how they habitually label their shyness. They may do so by using such words as 'I always feel awkward and tense when I'm with people', or 'I'm no good with strangers', or 'I can't cope with speaking in public', and go on from there to tell themselves 'This is because I'm a shy person' or 'This shows I can't help being shy'. This is an example of what psychologists call *circular reasoning*, and like all circular reasoning it places people in a Catch 22 situation.

Relabelling (a technique which is explained fully on page 79) breaks the circle. For example, the individual can be guided to say 'Being with people is a challenge, but the discomfort I feel is a sign I'm meeting the challenge'. Or 'When I meet strangers I'm a stranger to them too. So we both feel awkward at first, but that's merely part of getting to know each other'. To be successful, this relabelling requires persistence. All the situations in which the individual feels particularly shy must be searched out, and each of them relabelled adaptively and positively. The actual situations should be imagined taking place, as in the previous strategy, and the new label held in mind at the same time.

Shy people should also be reminded that other people are often not as confident as they appear. They're simply better at hiding how unsure of themselves they are. Crucially, shy people should also be reminded that others are rarely studying them as closely as they think, and that social inadequacies or physical imperfections which to them stand out a mile are often virtually unnoticeable to others. Since blushing and nervous sweating seem to be due to an upset in the body's natural thermostat (interestingly, people apparently don't blush when they're naked, no matter how embarrassed they may be feeling!) it makes sense also to remind them not to muffle themselves up too extravagantly when about to face a potentially difficult social situation.

SELF-ASSERTION

Self-assertion is one of the social problems most often faced by people in both their professional and personal lives. Many feel they'd like to give a better account of themselves. They find they sometimes back down from necessary conflict, they strive always to avoid 'unpleasant-ness'. They hesitate to express themselves, or to correct someone else's facts, or to speak out in public, or to admit when they don't understand something or somebody. They do not assert their rights, or refuse un-reasonable demands or let someone know when they're being difficult or offensive.

Problems related to self-assertion crop up not just in close relation-ships or in Level 4 professional relationships with senior colleagues (see page 33), but in contexts where one would least expect them, and it's here they sometimes present maximum difficulty. For instance, some people say that although they can stand up for themselves in Level 3 or 4 relationships, Levels 1, 2 and 5 are more of a problem. They find it hard to reprimand junior colleagues, or to be firm with clients, or to complain about poor service in shops, or to complain that someone's smoking or noise levels are intrusive.

Many people are of course taught from an early age not to speak up for themselves, or to complain too loudly, or to express their real thoughts or feelings. Though self-restraint is needed at times, the trouble is our conditioning can impose it upon us so rigorously that it becomes self-repression. Parents and teachers fail to see that the self-assertion necessary in effective adult life is often the very quality that can make us seem difficult when we're young. But unless this quality is allowed at sensible levels in children, it won't emerge magically in their adult lives at the precise moment when society suddenly starts to prize it.

A result of this conditioned self-repression is that we may grow up feeling we'll only gain approval if we always make a tremendous effort to be nice, self-effacing, polite, apologetic and co-operative, and avoid being outspoken, emotionally aroused, self-aware, and at times downright troublesome in the defence of our own and other people's rights. We spend so much time seeking approval and needing to be liked that we have no space left in which to explore who we really are, and to discover how we can develop into *really* acceptable and effective men and women.

Self-assertion as discussed here musn't be confused with arrogance or selfishness or insensitivity. As always, a balance is needed between personal needs and the needs of others. What it means is the freedom to be oneself without feeling guilty for it, the freedom to express personal needs with a realism similar to that with which one listens and responds to the needs of others, and the freedom to stand up for one's legitimate rights without the need to apologise for so doing.

☐ *Michael attended a social skills workshop with a number of problems, both personal and professional. One of these was that he worried over the often ineffectual way in which he tried to say what he really meant. In the course of role-play sessions, two of Michael's tasks were:*

1. *to complain to an equal status colleague (Level 3 relationship) that the latter had taken advantage of his absence on sick leave to purloin his secretary, leaving him with someone less efficient;*

2. *to inform a junior colleague (Level 2 relationship) that he was refusing her request for leave of absence at a busy time of year to attend the wedding of a distant cousin in the United States.*

In the first exercise Michael made repeated use of such questions as 'Don't you think you're being a bit unfair about this?' instead of relying on definite statements like 'You're being very unfair'. In the second exercise he interspersed his remarks with comments like 'I'm sorry about this', and 'I know how disappointed you must feel', instead of simply stating his decision and giving his reasons.

The other participants of the workshop felt that Michael was giving clear signals in the Level 3 relationship that he wasn't going to put up too much of a fight over the secretary, or take the issue to someone higher up, while in the Level 2 relationship he was signalling personal guilt, and giving advance permission for resentment and accusations. In the latter case, it was felt that he had no need to apologise for refusing what was a most unreasonable request. If anyone had a right to feel resentment, it was Michael for being put in the position of having to refuse.

Michael accepted these observations, and identified the source of his behaviour at Levels 2 and 3 as his own lack of conviction of his right to take up a firm position on any major issue. In the Level 3 relationship he confessed he would have the sneaking feeling that maybe his colleague would make better use of an efficient secretary than he was doing. And in the Level 2 relationship he would agonise over whether he was justified in denying someone the opportunity of such an exciting experience.

Once he acknowledged this, Michael saw his lack of self-conviction as unrealistic, since, objectively, he could recognise his own worth. He felt it had something to do with being the youngest of four high-achieving children. As a boy, he had been aware that whatever he did, there was always a sibling who could do it better, and who would criticise or belittle his efforts. Similarly, whenever he got into a debate, there was always a sibling who would scorn his arguments.

He was therefore encouraged to identify a broad sample of the situations in which his lack of self-conviction would arise, and to practise relabelling it as an old inappropriate response habit, and one which could safely be ignored as irrelevant to his life as he was actually experiencing it.

Relabelling, which was first discussed in connection with shyness on page 77, is a strategy which is often very valuable in helping individuals break out of inappropriate ways of responding. Essentially, it involves recognising that, often through conditioning, we have over a period of time been labelling a particular response or a particular emotion in a certain way without analysing whether the label is accurate (or helpful). The procedure is then to replace this label with a more suitable one. For example, we may routinely label a lack of self-assertion as 'politeness', whereas in fact it should be labelled as failure to claim our rights. Or we may label an emotion as fear of confrontation, when in fact it's the body gearing up to face challenge (physiologically fear and the excitement caused by challenge are very similar).

But to return to Michael. He offers a good instance of how some individuals hold themselves back in their relationships. His fear of failure, of laying himself open to criticism, of being disliked, meant that for much of the time he was not being what is sometimes called 'authentic'. That is, true to his real thoughts and feelings about his abilities and about the respect he deserves, and thus not allowing himself to give self and others a rounded and accurate picture of who he really is. He expressed this as 'a fear of being myself', not because there was anything wrong with being himself, but because that was the way his early experiences had taught him to behave.

The paradox behind all this holding back is that, as Michael himself observed, he had ended up not only less effective personally and socially, but also less attractive. He risked being dull and colourless. Other people may have described him as 'nice' and as 'always pleasant', but they were unlikely to want him as a role model, and unlikely to choose him as a leader or initiator. By trying too hard to make himself acceptable he had succeeded only in censoring out many of the very things about himself which would contribute most to this acceptability.

When self-assertion workshops first became popular some years ago, it was assumed that self-assertion was primarily a matter of standing up for ourselves and having our say. But it is now recognised this is simplistic. Self-assertion is essentially having the courage to accept and be the person we are, with all our strengths and weaknesses and individualities. It's the courage to believe in ourselves, and the confidence to convey this belief to others. It has nothing to do with exploiting others, or with always putting our own interests first.

SAYING 'NO'

Self-assertion sometimes involves saying 'no' to excessive or unreasonable demands – thus placing boundaries around our professional lives. To use ourselves effectively and efficiently, there are certain things we *can do*, certain things we *might do* if we have sufficient time or if there isn't anybody better placed than us to do them, and certain things we *can't do*. We therefore need to say 'yes' to the first group, 'yes' or 'no' depending on the circumstances to the second, and 'no' to the third.
   When you want to say 'no', it will help if you:

* rehearse the word – for some of us it's so unfamiliar it doesn't sound right! Try it out, in private and aloud;

* identify in advance the kind of requests that fall into the 'can't do' category, and be ready for them when they arise;

* prepare an appropriate refusal that is polite but firm and *starts* with 'no' ('No I'm sorry I'm having to refuse that kind of request'; 'No I'm not the best person to do that'; 'No that's not in my field');

* use a definite tone of voice – people can all too easily sense when you don't mean what you say;

* once you've said 'no', do not change your mind except in very special circumstances. If you get a reputation for backing down, people will work on you until you do;

- don't feel too guilty about saying 'no'. If you've worked out carefully the 'can't do' category, you should be confident that your refusal is justified;

- set boundaries upon your 'yes'. If you make clear the limits to which you're agreeing, people have fewer grounds for returning to pester you to do more and more.

STRESS AND RELAXATION

UNWINDING AFTER SOCIAL CONFLICT

Often the period *after* saying no and sticking to it, or the period *after* social conflict, is as bad as these experiences themselves. Even experienced professionals confess to feeling shaky and upset for hours or days afterwards, and to reliving over and over again each small detail of the encounter in question.

It's important to dwell sufficiently on a bad social experience to let yourself come to terms with it and learn useful lessons from it. But brooding will only increase your stress level. There are three useful rules for unwinding after social conflict. These are:

Reflect — Reward — Relax

Reflect means thinking about the experience constructively and objectively. Focus upon what actually happened, and not simply upon what you were feeling. Identify this feeling at the outset (anger? fear? injured pride? resentment at injustice?), but don't become so caught up in it that it hinders your objectivity and rekindles the feeling instead of helping lay it to rest. By focusing on what actually happened, you will be able to recognise what went wrong and why. How could it have been avoided? Was there anything you said or did that with hindsight could have been better done differently? When the same or similar situations occur in the future, how will you now be better equipped to deal with them? Could you have predicted the situation more accurately? Is there any way in which you could have avoided it or been better prepared for it? Is there any necessary follow-up, and if so what is it and how can it best be done?

You should reflect about the situation for as long, and only as long, as you can learn from it. Once lessons have been learnt, any further brooding will only prolong bad feelings, and might encourage you actually to enjoy probing your wounds (rather as your tongue will seek out a painful tooth). Or brooding might encourage you to nurse your resentment, and hatch plans for taking revenge on the person or persons concerned.

Reward means rewarding oneself, congratulating yourself on your performance. Many people say they've nothing to be very proud about in the way they handled things. The reply to this is to stress the value of a positive approach. Certainly there are things to be proud about. However bad the encounter was, you came through it. And in the process of reflection mentioned above you will have identified a number of factors which will help you be better prepared for similar encounters in the future.

There will also have been some more specific positive things about your performance, if you look for them. Maybe you kept your temper that bit longer than usual; or kept more closely to the point; or were more positive; or made an effort to compromise; or tried to lower the temperature. We are most of us quick to blame ourselves for our social shortcomings, but we rarely congratulate ourselves for the things we improve upon or get right ('Well at least I did better than that awful time when . . . ').

So reward yourself. Tell yourself, in the words you'd use to praise someone else, that you're pleased with how things went and have learnt from them, that you're pleased that you did your best in terms of how you felt at the time. It's easy enough, with the security of hindsight, to look back at how we coped with a difficult situation and see what we *should* have done. But being in the middle of the situation and thinking about it later are two very different things. In the stress of the moment you did the best you could, and that is reason for congratulation.

Give yourself a tangible reward too sometimes – something special for the evening meal, or a trip to the cinema or the theatre, or even an early night in bed with a good book. Whatever it is, choose something that makes it clear to yourself that you deserve thanks, and that you're confident that next time you'll do even better as a result of what you've learnt from today's episode.

Relax means letting go of the physical and psychological stress that lingers after a social confrontation. Check yourself physically for signs of tension. Sit or lie comfortably, and let your awareness sweep slowly down your body. Is there tension in the forehead? In the neck? In the shoulders? In the back? In the belly? And so on down through the body. As you become aware of any tensions, let them go. This letting go may not happen at once.

Help the relaxation process by giving your mind something peaceful to think about in place of the events of the day. Concentrate upon your breathing. Put your hand on your abdomen and breathe from as low down as you can. Don't interfere too much with the rhythm of your breathing, but slow it down and deepen it a little. Take pleasure in the even rise and fall of the diaphragm.

Another useful aid is visualisation. Visualise an imaginary or a familiar scene which for you symbolises peace and relaxation. Imagine yourself there. Feel the warmth of the sun on your face, and hear the sound of the sea or of the birds or of the wind in the trees. Look at the colours and the shapes and the graceful way in which nature arranges herself. Draw in the peace of the scene with each breath and become one with it. Stay with the scene as long as you like. Once a relaxation exercise of this kind has become established, you can refresh yourself with it even at the most stressful times, closing your eyes for a moment and focusing on your breathing and then on your favourite place of inner peace.

Once you feel more relaxed, don't allow the mind to return to its worries of the day. Remember there are good days and there are bad days, and they all pass just the same. The bad days may leave an unpleasant taste, but the events of tomorrow will soon begin to dilute it, and leave us wondering before long what all the fuss was about. These points are dealt with more fully in my book *Managing Stress* (1989; this series).

HANDLING STRESSFUL FEELINGS

There are other ways of relaxing after stressful professional encounters of course. Physical activity can be a great help. So can the company of friends (though cultivate the habit of being at peace with your own mind, without always relying on others to distract you from yourself). So can solitude (though don't always go off on your own and shun others). It's a help to have family or confidants with whom you can talk over your problems when you wish. But the emphasis here is upon *when you wish*. Some psychologists give the impression it's only psychologically healthy if you always want to talk about your problems. This is an oversimplification. Many individuals prefer to leave the working day behind them at the end of the afternoon, and this serves them pretty well. So there's no reason why they should force themselves to share the disasters of the day with their partner the moment they arrive home. The moral for us all is to share these stories when it helps, and forget them when it doesn't.

However, don't slip into the habit of not being able to talk about your problems. We all need practice from time to time at unburdening ourselves. Talking about our problems helps to keep us open to others, to be ready to ask for help and a sympathetic ear when necessary, and to be more flexible about who was right and who was wrong. It also allows those close to us to see that we accept our fallibility, and to help us think problems through properly and offer advice and opinions.

For some people, the need to express and release feelings while unwinding is so great that they find it helps to pummel a cushion as a substitute for the person who aroused these feelings earlier in the day. The best advice to people who need this kind of release (and we all do sometimes) is, don't be afraid to be 'childish' about it. Go into a room on your own and jump up and down in rage just as a child would. Or weep floods of tears. Or shout 'No I *won't* do it' or 'I hate you', or whatever words express how you feel. Notice how good children are at releasing their feelings, and then turning their attention blissfully to other things. Watch a child arguing with a brother or sister. One moment it looks as if they're about to tear each other to pieces, and the next it's over and done with and they're great friends again. Strong feelings need a form of harmless release, and once they find it mind and body can settle into equanimity again.

Conclusion

This book has been about the social skills that allow us to get on with others in professional life. But it's also been about getting on with ourselves. Most people who understand and accept themselves tend to understand and accept others. A great psychologist once told us to love our neighbours as ourselves. Not 'instead of ourselves' or 'more than ourselves', but as ourselves. The implication behind these words is that love does not have boundaries between self and others. If we are able to grasp something of what it means to be wholly human, then we're also able to grasp that our neighbours (whether students, clients, colleagues or workers) are ultimately very like ourselves. They have many of the same hopes and dreams and fears, and, though we may each of us have rather different ways of hiding our wounds, they feel pain just as we do. We're also able to grasp that we're very much like *them*, and are worthy of the same respect and consideration by virtue of it.

In studying ourselves we're therefore also studying others, and in studying others we're studying ourselves. Each of us is unique, and yet each of us is part of one another. Sympathy, empathy, and the bonds of caring and of compassion stem from a realisation of this self-evident truth. Whether we like it or not, and whether we think the idea is fanciful or not, we're companions on a journey. And like any companions, it pays us to look after each other.

Index

Managing Stress

David Fontana

Stress in professional life is a much discussed problem nowadays. Clearly, people under too much stress (or too little) do not work at their best. *Managing Stress* demonstrates the importance of identifying exactly what stresses you, including both external factors in the environment and factors within yourself. Using non-technical language, and with an emphasis upon practical and easily mastered strategies, David Fontana takes the reader step-by step through the things that can be done to enhance stress resistance and to increase professional efficiency.

Paperback 0 901715 97 2
Hardback 0 901715 98 0

Interviewing

Glynis M. Breakwell

Whether you are dealing with clients, patients or students, interviewing skills are employed in any situation where information is exchanged and evaluated: recruitment, appraisal, teaching skills, allocation resources, planning changes, dealing with the media. So what makes a good interview? There is more to it than asking and answering questions. Breakwell describes interviews from both perspectives - that of interviewer and interviewee - since to be effective you need to understand what is happening from both sides. Exercises and guidelines throughout the book are designed to promote self-assessment, to uncover stereotypes and misconceptions, and to try out the methods and skills described.

Paperback 1 85433 000 4
Hardback 1 85433 001 2

Psychology in Action Series

Psychology has a great deal to say about how we can make our working lives more effective and rewarding: the way we see other people, how they see us, and our ability to communicate with others and achieve what we want from a situation. 'Psychology in Action' looks at the everyday working methods and concerns of particular groups of people and asks: where and how can psychology help?

From the 'Psychology in Action' Series:

Classroom Control
David Fontana

0 901715 39 5 pb
0 901715 42 5 hb

Law in Practice
Sally Lloyd-Bostock

0 901715 66 2 pb
0 901715 67 0 hb

Police Work
Peter B. Ainsworth and Ken Pease

0 901715 44 1 pb
0 901715 45 X hb

Counselling and Helping
Stephen Murgatroyd

0 901715 41 7 pb

Nursing in the Community
Susan P. Llewelyn and Dennis R. Trent

0 901715 56 5 pb
0 901715 57 3 hb

Working with Children and their Families
Martin Herbert

0 901715 80 8 pb
0 901715 79 4 hb